Dork Whore

Dork Whore

My Travels Through Asia
as a Twenty-Year-Old Pseudo-Virgin

Iris Bahr

BLOOMSBURY

Author's note: The names and identifying characteristics of
some of the people in this story have been changed.

Published by Bloomsbury USA, New York
Distributed to the trade by Holtzbrinck Publishers

All papers used by Bloomsbury USA are natural, recyclable products
made from wood grown in well-managed forests. The manufacturing
processes conform to the environmental regulations of the country of
origin.

Library of Congress Cataloging-in-Publication Data

Bahr, Iris.
    Dork whore : my travels through Asia as a twenty-year-old pseudo-
virgin / Iris Bahr.—1st U.S. ed.
       p. cm.
    ISBN-13: 978-1-59691-234-2
    1. Bahr, Iris. 2. Bahr, Iris—Travel—Asia. 3. Asia—Description and
travel. 4. Actors—United States—Biography. I. Title.
    PN2287.B138A3 2006
    915.04'43092—dc22
    [B]
                                                          2006018506

First U.S. Edition 2007

1 3 5 7 9 10 8 6 4 2

Typeset by Westchester Book Group
Printed in the United States by Quebecor World Fairfield

A Note from the Author

These are the true chronicles of my search for sex in Asia. Some things have been slightly skewed for both protective and comedic purposes, i.e., people's names have been changed, the dialogue is not verbatim, and there are several descriptions which have arisen from slightly fuzzy memory. I'll tell you what they are now, so you won't have to question them later: the Aeroflot mango bit, the second Phat Phong visit, the Nam and Poonhill smoking sessions, Freddie's rabbit nuggets, the last day in Dharamsalah, and the extent of Tomer's hand job. That's it. The rest happened pretty much as festively messed-up as described, sex-fruit and shul trauma included.

—Iris Bahr
2007

Thailand

Chapter One

"**Kohmpehmentaree orchid!**" **she** barks, thrusting it up my nose with unnecessary vigor. I turn to Boaz. His slumbering logbody seems unperturbed by the disturbance, his mushy face still glued to a yellow travel pillow. His complimentary orchid, however, is dangling precariously from his chin, hanging on for dear life on the power of drool alone.

Ew.

"We're here," I say, lightly tapping the edge of his pinky. He lets out a wet snort and jolts upright with sausagey might, sending the orchid flying as the salivary support-bridge retracts into his cavernous mouth. He smiles a smelly smile at me, and despite all the grossness of his visage, I can't help smiling back.

We've arrived.

Boaz and I met six months ago at the Tel-Aviv Backpacker Store, a known pick-up joint for sole souls in need of travel companions. Like me, most of them were recently discharged soldiers wanting emotio-physical release after three years of puke-green uniforms, AK-47s, and chains of command. (Personally, I didn't mind the uniform; it made my ass look good.)

From my initial conversation with Boaz, it quickly became

apparent that he was both chubby and responsible. With much enthusiasm he described the special medicine bag he would provide for our journey, equipped with everything from antidiarrheals to emergency inhalers, lest we contract some sudden-onset respiratory disorder. And so we eagerly agreed to travel together and spent the next few months getting inoculated and buying film.

My mother was thrilled. She'd been in a concealed state of panic ever since she heard of my exotic travel plans and had been presenting various alternatives on a daily basis. Her suggestion to "Go to the Dead Sea for the weekend instead" had almost brought us to blows. I'd been forced to remind her that I'd sacrificed a coveted army post near Lebanon just so I could be stationed close to home and keep her company for two years. In short, we both knew this trip was mine. I also knew her concern was perfectly legitimate, and I was glad my particular choice of travel companion alleviated her anxiety. As far as she was concerned, Boaz was the perfect chaperone for her little girl about to roam Asia: a physically repulsive, medically well-stocked cockblocker.

Not that I need one. A cockblocker that is. Sex has scared the fuck out of me—literally. I have only had it once, and that was only kind of. He was a Moroccan paratrooper, oddly named Patrick. We had met on my base one cold night, two years ago. I had been on guard duty, Uzi slung over my shoulder, freezing my virginal ass off, when a form suddenly emerged from among the eucalyptus trees—a masculine form donning a red paratrooper beret, full combat gear, *and* hot body to boot. I couldn't believe my eyes. Such a fine specimen was unheard of in these parts. After all, my base was comprised entirely of Intelligence units, meaning the only men stationed there were very brilliant and very ugly. A real soldier like Patrick was God.

Which is why I knew I had to snatch this fine paratrooping creature before that hot chick in Libya Division got wind of him.

And so with much alacrity, I frisbeed a flirty comment through the barbed-wire gate as Patrick walked past, stopping him in his tracks. By sunrise he was smitten, and three weeks of dating bliss later I knew I'd finally found my cherry popper. Thank God. By that point I was the only virgin left among my friends. Among my unit. Among the entire base for that matter.

I was still getting my sex ed from Judy Blume.

It had gotten to the point where even just hanging out with the other girls in my unit made me uncomfortable. I found it much safer to just watch them from afar, as they'd congregate on the grassy patch by the flagpole and talk about how horny they were after being away from their boyfriends for so long. How they sent their boyfriends care packages with cookies and sexy notes to ease their stressful patrols along the casbahs of Jenin and Ramallah. How lucky they were to have boyfriends that were so virile they managed to overcome their military exhaustion and fuck them forty-six times last Saturday.*

Once in a confident while, I'd join them on the grassy patch, determined to just observe and learn. But it never quite worked out that way.

---

*I, too, had dated soldiers who patrolled the various casbahs of the West Bank and Gaza, but our weekends consisted not of sex and baked goods, but of me listening to harrowing tales of them dodging ovens, refrigerators, and other large kitchen appliances routinely thrown at them off of unwelcoming Palestinian rooftops.

"Hey, Iris, come join us!" Tamar would say. Tamar was a pretty, blue-eyed sweetheart with a remarkably feminine buzz cut.

"Okay," I'd reply, joining the group with apprehension and longing.

At this point, Dannah, the curly-haired vixen, would satanically light a cigarette. She was the one I was afraid of.

"You ever notice how these trees smell like cum?" she'd ask.

"What?" I'd reply, completely caught off guard.

"You mean you can't smell it?" Tamar would gasp, pointing to the seven eucalyptus trees looming over us. I'd take a deep breath.

All I smelled was artichoke.

But I wasn't about to miss out on this festive discussion. "Yeah . . . wow!" I'd say, still not sure whether cum smell was a good thing or not. "It does smell like cum, wow . . . yeah!"

"My boyfriend's cum doesn't smell like that," Sharon would chime in. Sharon was a rich girl from Jerusalem who had a nice house and great skin.

"Well, you're lucky!" the girls would retort with giggly sincerity.

"How about you, Iris, what do you think cum smells like?"

"Um . . . I don't know what cum smells like . . . I'm always too busy swallowing it."

Hysterical laughter would then ensue among the estrogen unit, whereupon I'd quietly race back into the building, lest the conversation got more detail-oriented.

How I longed for the day I'd be able to speak with knowledge and grace about smelly fluids found in nature. My hope was that now, thanks to Patrick, that day would be coming soon. Preferably no later than next Tuesday.

I gave Patrick the imminent-deflowering news over dinner at the Hard Rock Café.* He was overjoyed.

"Don't worry," he assured me. "I'm well endowed—even by Moroccan standards!"

He wasn't kidding. And I'm talking knowledge through pain. The man was so huge, I was only able to tolerate his presence inside me for several seconds. Deenie had not prepared me for this scudlike scenario. The slut.†

With strained forehead I requested an immediate pull-out, which for some reason was only granted a full pumpy minute later (apparently Patrick didn't hear my request the first three times), whereupon I lay in his arms in intense postcoital shivering.

I apologized, assuring Patrick that we would try again and make it work. He caressed my hair, gently whispering in my ear that "It wasn't a problem," and that he planned on "spending more time in Jerusalem with his girlfriend anyway," and in actuality, they were "going to move in together later that month." And with that, he promptly packed up his Moroccan member and took off, leaving me to shiver my shock out alone.

* * *

---

*Which has since been bombed to bits. I think there's a pharmacy there now.
†Deenie had been my most trusted Blume source, making her lack of counsel especially hurtful.

Needless to say, nightmares of eternal hymenization have followed. The way I see it today, my poonani has become my own personal Gaza Strip: against occupation, yet lost without it; unable to get past the partial-penetration stage; wanting nothing more than a stable infrastructure, a proper sewage system, and maybe, one day, even a rec center.

But none of the potential penetrators will do. They're either impatient assholes, boring chubsters, or oversensitive doormats that smell weird. I've gotten so skilled at detecting flaws, I can find at least five completely legitimate reasons for dumpage within the first ten seconds of an encounter, long before sex is even proposed (well, actually, *right* before it's proposed. The men move fast in Tel-Aviv).

But this efficiency has only made me more anxious, for every passing day has further dimmed the light at the end of my bio-tunnel, leaving me a with a virginal hang-up so enormous I've insta-dumped every potential penetrator in the greater Tel-Aviv area. My friends, in contrast, couldn't be more sexually active or annoying and I find myself falling further into the abyss of bitterness, self-pity, and hatred.

I've finally concluded that the only way for me to break free from this oppressive state of frustrated flowerdom is to clean my slate, i.e., go somewhere so foreign and transformational I could forget my own history.

Asia.

Chapter Two

Bangkok International welcomes us by losing Boaz's bags. Apparently they are "en route to Cyprus, but will be delivered to your guesthouse by next Tuesday." Boaz enters fitville. "This is not an airline conspiracy to sabotage your luggage and sanity," I tell him, but he just stares at me blankly, refusing to move even an inch from the information counter. I finally manage to extricate him from the formica with the help of a scowling airline employee, and together we drag him kicking and screaming toward the terminal exit.

Boaz and I step outside and take our first hungry inhale of fresh air, only to have our nasal passages raped by a sticky aromatic soup of fish, sweat, sewage, dead cats, and cologne, as if the entire city were belching up a horrible meal at two-second intervals.

Thankfully, a passing taxicab swallows our desperate bodies and we head toward the main backpacker drag known as Kao San Road. My animated attempts at distracting Boaz with the exciting scenery quickly prove futile. In fact, he's still whimpering about his lost meds as we arrive at Kao San Road two hours later.

Taking his hand, I maneuver us through the dried fish racks, Buddhist monks, stray dogs, pirated music vendors, and Calvin Klein sportswear stands, finally arriving at the Melody Guesthouse, one of several establishments lauded by the *Lonely Planet* travel guide.*

As we check into a tiny, wood-paneled room reminiscent of the Brady Bunch foyer, I make a final effort to raise Boaz's spirits, appealing this time to his more primal needs.

"Whaddya say we go grab some Thai food!"

With a heavy sigh, Boaz and his imposed burden descend onto the flimsy mattress, which, in turn, painfully sinks into the frail metal bedframe, pushing through the coils with a slow, doomful squeal.

"No, that's all right," Boaz mumbles. "I think I'll just take a nap . . . I mean . . . (*laborious pause*) . . . It's not like I have anything to unpack . . . or anything (*chest clutch*) . . ."

Boaz raises his head carefully, lest it break off his neck in agonizing self-pity. I realize I have a stupid *Eating can be fun!* smile on my face.

"Okay! See you later!" I yelp, managing a bright salute as I exit back into the colorful sludge of Kao San Road.

I spot an eatery called Thai World and eagerly enter the haven of soy-flavored air-conditioning. Service is not the swiftest at Thai World, and I wait for an eternity before a hairless ruffian finally hands me a menu. I grab it with glee, keen to scan the local offerings. But the closest thing I find to Pad Thai on the menu is BLT on wheat.

And so I order two Jew-haters and a banana shake. My order arrives two full episodes of *Sanford and Son* later (simultaneously screened on three TV sets suspended from various parts of the ceiling), but is well worth the wait. Who

---

*The backpacker's bible.

knew the Asians made such a good sandwich? Satiated, I
head back to the guesthouse in good spirits. They quickly
diminish, however, when it dawns on me that our room has
only one bed. And not a very large one at that. I only pray
Boaz has already fallen asleep, thereby allowing me to angle
a position on the bed that's far enough from him to politely
hint, "Don't touch me, you're disgusting," but at the same
time give me enough room to spread my arms and legs in
my preferred T-like fashion.

A new morning. I'm relieved to report Boaz is in much better spirits. We've just enjoyed some sumptuous Reubens at
Thai World and are walking back to the Melody to pick up
my camera, when Boaz abruptly steps onto the street and
hails down a cab.

"What are you doing?" I ask, confused.

"I'm going to the airport."

"Why? The airline said they'd deliver your bags to the
guesthouse."

"No, I'm leaving."

"Leaving?"

"Yes, Thailand is not what I expected. It's too dirty. And
I have insufficient medications. I'm going to Paris instead."

"Paris?! What are you talking about? We planned this trip
for months—you can't just go to Paris! What about me?"

"I'm sorry, I already changed my ticket last night. Good
luck and be safe."

And with that, he enters his chariot of salvation and
rides off.

I remain frozen on the curb. An air plume of dogfish wafts
past, catalyzing my shock into panic. Six months of mutual

planning and inoculations, and here I am, barely a day in this crazy city, alone and medless.

Fuck.

I rush back to the stuffy womby comfort of the room, lay on the bed in full T formation, and begin to masturbate in a vain effort to ease my anxiety. My finger, jittery and tense, keeps missing its mark, and I finally get so frustrated at its lack of focus that I start smacking it into the pillow, wishing it were Boaz's head I was thwacking instead.

It's been four hours since my little outburst and I find myself still splattered on the bed, paralyzed. If I have to stare at this fucking wood paneling for one more second I'm going to scream. I'm also not thrilled about the insanely sharp pain that just hit my abdomen. That can mean only one thing: shit. As in, I need to. Badly.

Down the hallway I scurry in search of the facilities. The "water closet" turns out to be a hole in the ground lined with pink tile. Nice touch. I quickly de-pant, crouch, and in one fell swoop let out all the BLTs, anxiety, and airline peanuts I've consumed over the last twenty-four hours. The whole procedure takes half a second, as if my bowels were being timed on a stopwatch.

I reach over to grab some toilet paper, but in its stead find a snaky showerhead thingie. I see . . . the Thai don't *wipe* it out, they *wash* it out. Nifty. I carefully angle the showerhead under me and press the lever. The jet stream shoots out like a missile and sends me flying into the wall, in the process cleaning every piece of microscopic debris that's inhabited my rectum since I was two. I leap up off the cold tile, hoping the three-second rule also applies to bacteria-to-butt contact, and haul my immaculate asshole back to Thai World.

After all, I have to find a new travel mate, quick. Either that, or catch the next shuttle to Pompidou, and I'm not quite ready for that.

Yet.

Chapter Three

This whole "meeting people" endeavor is proving to be difficult. I've been sitting here at Thai World for hours, trying to look as cute and available as possible, but they are not even glancing my way. And by *they* I mean every Goddamn person in here. *They* are all sitting in these tight-knit groups, a weathered "we already trekked the Himalayas together" familiarity among them.

Damn Boaz for leaving me here like this.

I bite hungrily into my BLT (what can I say, they're addictive—I have yet to taste a bamboo shoot), hoping my eating activity will somehow create a wall between me and my self-consciousness. But four sandwiches later, I'm still fully aware of being invisible. I think I've met my self-torture quota for one night. Let's face it. I'm just a clean-assed loser with a pork problem waiting to be noticed. Time to head back to the station wagon.

I'm wiping a stray piece of breaded sin off my face when a raspy voice slinks up behind me.

"Slow down!" he says.

I freeze. Could it be? Was someone talking to me? I turn around and encounter a massive mountain of squiggly hair.*

---

*Also known as the "Isra-fro." The Isra-fro is a syndromal phenomenon of Israeli postmilitary freedom. Having endured three or more years of regulations

It's Yoni, some Israeli guy from our flight. Definitely not a contender for the penetrator plan, but a welcome human interaction nonetheless. His voice is an odd combination of enthused confidence and laid-back tranquility, as if he knows what you're going to say before you say it, but is fascinated by the information just the same.

"Hey, Yoni! How are you?" I say, hugging him as if we were old buddies.

"I'm doing fantastic. Where's Boaz?"

"Paris."

"Great!"

Am I the only one who finds this turn of events shocking?

"What are your plans tonight, Iris?"

"I was just gonna go back to my room and masturbate for a few hours in sheer panic and then call my mom and tell her what a great time Boaz and I are having."

"Oh."

By now I've gathered that Yoni is not the brightest detector of sarcasm. Then again, I'm not sure I was being sarcastic.

"What are your plans, Yoni?" I ask, figuring direct questions would avoid confusion and lost humor.

"Well, I'm leaving for India tomorrow and wanted to catch a hard-core sex show in Phat Phong tonight before I go. Wanna come?" he asks, adjusting his fro to the left.

"Sure!" I exclaim, grateful for the human company, but

_____cont'd

and buzz cuts, 99.9 percent of Israeli men grow their hair out immediately upon discharge, regardless of how curly, horrible, or demented their locks reveal themselves to be. And so the streets are filled with scores of Israeli men sporting electrocuted bushes, if you will, that they sometimes attempt to subdue into bulky ponytails, but usually leave wild. The ironic result of this outburst of self-expression and rebellion is an Israeli tribe of fro-clones.

even more so for this promising preface to my sexual eman-
cipation.

Who would've thought the skankiest sex clubs in the world
were nestled in the confines of a family-friendly flea market?
Talk about perfect marketing. Here at the Phat Phong one can
get one's kicks and gifts out of the way in one easy evening!

As Yoni and I make our way through the market, he informs me that we're going to a heterosexual paradise mis-
leadingly named the Queens Club, the only club without a
cover charge.

To his impatient dismay, I stop and purchase a pair of
nifty bronze sun-and-moon candlesticks.

"Can't it wait till later?" he implores, alerting me to the
numerous possible misunderstandings involved in entering
a sex club with two long metal objects. But I've already
haggled the lady down to two hundred baht and am not
about to leave empty-handed. So I complete the transaction
and, armed with my phallic double-duty entendres, follow
Yoni up the stairs into the club.

We're led directly to the front row. I take my seat and
lean back, trying to appear cool and comfortably nonvir-
ginal. Across the way sit a group of pasty tassle-loafered
Germans, unabashedly kneading the breasts of some giggly
Thai girls who are sitting on their laps sucking on lollipops.

The lights dim and Depeche Mode starts playing on the
system ("People Are People," an old favorite). A naked
woman crawls on stage and begins to pour hot wax on
herself.

"I told you these would come in handy!" I say, lifting the
candlesticks up in offering. But Yoni yanks my arm down,

and we watch as the woman proceeds to her next number: opening a non-twist-off beer bottle with her vagina.

Very soon other props are brought into the fold: Arrows. Balloons. Cigarettes. Disgust. Terror. Titillation. Before I can cheer, "Go Kegel!" a peeled banana has disappeared into her cavernous insides. THE WHOLE THING. *Poof!* Just like that.

Mastervag slinks farther down the stage and winks at me seductively. Many a mature woman would be intimidated by this hypersexed situation, but not me. Noooo sir. My left eyelid slowly descends in reciprocal affection, but before it completes its journey, I suddenly notice a nasty smirk form on Mastervag's face. I look to Yoni, who grabs my hand nervously. I'm confused. What's going on?

BAM!

The banana launches itself from within her diseased innards and flies straight at me at 45 mph. Yoni tries to pull me out of the way, but it's too late. The banana smacks me right in the mouth, which opens in shock, enabling some sweet-and-sour shmutz to creep in. I race to the bathroom and frantically flood the contaminated area with amoebic tap water.

Despite my protests, Coach Yoni drags me away from the sink and back out toward the exit. As we pass the stage, he lifts my arm in victory, spurring some patronly applause and a loud cry of *"Goooalllll!"* from the Germans. They're beaming, in awe of the girl lucky enough to have sipped the juice they have to pay to taste. I manage a faint bow of accomplishment. Their acceptance feels oddly satisfying, as if I've somehow climbed up a notch on the sexual status scale. After all, I just discovered the milk and honey of the underworld—the banana-coochie shake.

Chapter Four

I'm up ridiculously early this morning, thanks to my trusty bowel alarm clock.* Not that I managed to sleep much anyway—I was too busy worrying about where I could get an AIDS test after last night's fruit fest. I know, it's pointless getting tested so soon after exposure, not to mention the fact that the chances of being infected by fruit are pretty slim, but one must also remember that the woman's insides were directly inserted into my mouth at great velocity. Besides, AIDS testing falls under the category of "Types of Activities Sexually Active People Engage In," and any opportunity to be part of that category needs to be taken advantage of.

It dawns on me that Yoni is halfway to Bombay by now, and so I venture off to the hospital alone, too preoccupied with my potential state of health to fret over solitude.

The emergency room at what the Lonely Planet guide calls the "Best Hospital in Bangkok" is completely deserted. Not even a courtesy bell. Since my Thai lingual skills are limited to "BLT on wheat" and "Kao San Road," I'm hoping the employees here speak English—wherever they may

---

*Available in both digital and analog models.

be. I accordingly prep my hyperloud, grammatically flawed special English for foreigners.

"HALLO? IS THERE A PERSON IN HOSPITAL HERE?"

A mousy woman sporting a crisp white uniform and dirty green flip-flops scurries her way toward me.

"What you need?" she pelts.

"AIDS test."

"HIV?"

"Yes."

"Very popular."

Is that supposed to cheer me up?

"Thirty minute for result."

How on earth could a test that requires two weeks to process anywhere else in the world take only half an hour here? That's absurd! Then again, I *am* in the AIDS capital of the world—they obviously know what they're doing. Then again, I *am* in the AIDS capital of the world—they obviously have no idea what they're doing.

Well, I've got nothing to lose besides some blood, really, so I relinquish my arm to the mercy of her needlepoint skills, then rush to the bathroom, where I expertly jet-stream my anxiety out my rear end.

I return to the deserted waiting area and peruse the crusty Thai periodical I spotted earlier. Less than five minutes transpire before Sister Doogie comes scuffling back down the hallway—her right flip-flop disintegrating further and further with each step, leaving a nice trail of crumbled green rubber behind her.

"You okay," she says, expressionless.

"Uh . . . thank you," I reply, wondering if she determined my HIV status on intuition alone.

"No problem," she replies. "Be fun."

"Thanks. You . . . uh . . . be fun, too."

Thank God. Out of the hospital and back on a *tuk-tuk*, riding through the deoxygenated city streets. Though I can't call what we're doing "riding" really, considering we've been at a complete standstill for over forty minutes. My tuk-tuk driver has thoughtfully positioned us so that my mouth is two inches away from the neighboring truck's exhaust pipe. The truck driver keeps pressing on the gas pedal, as if entertained by the sight of black smoke forcing its way into my AIDS-free lungs.

I wonder what Boaz is doing right now. Probably eating a baguette in some overly manicured park, apologizing for his Jewishness to some French fuck named Laurent.

As if *I* were better off: alone in this congested abyss of decadence and deathfruit, feeling nothing but dirty, rejected, and—considering my sudden craving for a banana shake—possibly gay.

There's no way this sex-and-smog bacchanal is all that Thailand has to offer. It can't be. After all, the Lonely Planet dedicated about 150 pages to the northern countryside, a magical land of elephant treks and friendly locals, of exotic cultures and nifty handicrafts. That's obviously where I need to get to. And you know what? That's where I'm going. Enough hanging around this sticky shithole. I'm off to see the real Thailand—travel partner or no travel partner!

But first I have to call my mommy, which can be done at a reasonable rate at the Happy Times Phone Center. The fact that I haven't called her four times since daybreak and have yet to be reported as missing is a miracle. She usually masks her worry with gushing enthusiasm, lots of happy yelling, and sudden tearful eruptions over how much she loves me, all of which make me feel incredibly guilty for just being alive and consequently the cause of such concern and affection. A normal youth would recognize this dynamic as crazy and not succumb to the demand to notify the world they're okay on an hourly basis. But such a rational way of being is beyond my grasp, and every second my mother is not alerted of my well-being, I'm tortured by the fear that she'll collapse in grief over the unknown current state of her offspring. Such is the fate of a quasi–only child.

Ring ring.

Hi, Ima, it's me. Yes, me, Iris. Ima—Ima—DON'T YELL IMA, I can hear you . . . *Yes*! Yes, the connection is perfect . . . yes . . . what? We're having a great time . . . Actually I *have* been eating enough fruit, yes. We're heading up north in an hour. Well, it's uh . . . a midnight tour. Organized, of course, of course. Okay, Ima, I'll call you in three days . . . What? I don't know what time exactly . . . Fine, two days. Well, I just don't know if I'll be able to find a phone up there. No, no, of course I can find a phone. You're right. Tomorrow. Okay. I love you, too. Yes. Love you. Okay. Okay. Okay. I have to go Ima . . . because Boaz is getting hungry. Yes, he's right here next to me. I will tell him you said hi. I love you, too. Okay. Ima, stop. Tomorrow. Okay, I gotta go. Bye!

Chapter Five

This midnight bus ride to Chiang Mai is not the social fiesta I was hoping it would be. It's just like Thai World only dark and bumpy. I've been staring into windowed nothingness for hours. We have, however, just pulled up to a fluorescent oasis, a truck stop of sorts, where the main items for sale are fish rinds and massive blocks of generic Cracker Jack wrapped in cellophane. I quietly disembark, purchase a Coke and two blocks of Jack, and return self-consciously to my seat.

I take a needy bite out of my sugarbrick and promptly crack a tooth. Wonderful. I'm grabbing my Coke to wash the blood down when suddenly I spot a gorgeous guy through the window. Ridiculously gorgeous. How did I not see him before? Tall, broad shoulders, bushy brown hair, sculpted jaw, full lips, a sexual swagger, an inkling in my loins. Good God. This is the man I've been waiting for, my stomach can't deny it.

Oooh. He's about to board the bus! What do I do now? Do I invite him to sit next to me? Do we go fuck behind the deli for a little bit? (Can one fuck for just a "little bit?") He probably thinks I'm twelve years old, hunched over in my seat like this, hugging my Cracker Jack, trying to hide the tiny love puddle that's formed beneath me.

Oh shit, he's on the bus now. He's even hotter up close. He takes a seat one row in front of me. A moment later he's joined by a white barrel of a man, who's wearing the thickest tequila shot glasses I've ever seen. His face is also home to a grotesque, horsey grin. Introducing the "Ugly Friend." Every hottie has one. Ugly people should have them, too, considering the wonders they do for one's self-esteem. In fact, I could use an ugly friend myself right about now.

From their sepia teeth I safely conclude that these men are Her Majesty's subjects. I lean in for a little listen. Yep, their speech confirms it. Right now they're reminiscing over their time in Kuala Lumpur last January. Apparently they've been traveling for over a year. Wow. Why would they waste their time with a fresh loser like me? Oh come on, woman. That kind of attitude isn't going to help you. You're a charming person in your own right. You spent two years in the Israeli military. You're a bad ass. You can be funny. And you're horny. You definitely have some perks.

"Excuse me?" I whisper gently.

They keep talking. Ignoring me already. Great.

Deep breath. Try again.

"EXCUSE ME!" I blout,* unintentionally sounding impatient, abrasive, and disgusted.

Hottie turns around, somewhat taken aback at my outrage. His profile is nothing short of magnificent.

I bat an eyelash but have a feeling it looks more like a seizure.

"Is there a problem?" he asks, quizzically.

"Uh . . . no. Hi! I just overheard you blokes saying you were on your way to trek in Chiang Mai, and I was

---

*The ole shout and blurt combo. My specialty.

wondering if I could . . . um . . . possibly *join* you. Perhaps. If you don't mind. If it's not a bother."

Silence.

Hottie looks over at Horsie. If only I could see their faces. My stomach does a triple axle. Why the hell am I so nervous? What's the worse they could say—"No"? Oh God, I would die if they said no.

"No problem."

Whew.

"I'm Johnny," Hottie announces. Those lips.

We stare in each other's eyes for a moment. If he keeps this up, I'm gonna flood the bus. Horsie turns around to see what all the dripping is about.

"I'M HUGH!" he shouts, his voice even outbigging his eyes.

"I'm Iris," I reply nervously, unable to unlock my gaze from Johnny's.

"Guinness?"

"No. Ee-reese. Like Iris, but different."

"Ahh. Irisssssssss. What kind of name is that?" he says, licking his lips.

"Israeli."

"I see. So you'll join us for a few days then, Irissss."

"I'd love to," I reply, a flood of relief washing over me. But wait. Did he just say "a few days"? Does that mean they know they're going to get sick of me after a few days? Or have I gotten so paranoid that my ability to take offense manages to precede the arrival of the actual insult?

"A few days sounds perfect, Johneeeeeee."

We share a rippling laugh. Part truth, part invitation. I can feel myself scoring some points. Johnny turns all the way around to face me.

"I'm sure you're a tough chick, having been in the army, yes?"

"Yeah, what kind of fighting did you do?" Hugh chimes in.

They both look at me expectantly.

Now the dilemma. Do I play up the army card and tell them I could kick their English pussy asses with my Krav Maga skills and AK-47 precision shot, or do I tell them the truth: that I basically spent my mandatory two-year military service listening in on various Intelligence feeds in a tiny office ten minutes away from my house, and that I couldn't even thumb wrestle without losing my breath? A lot is at stake here. I need to impress. But do I have to lie?

I take a dramatic, brow-furrowed inhale.

"I can't really talk about the army. I'm sorry."

They both nod in solemn comprehension. Perfect. I've left it up to them to conjure images of me in stilettos toting a Kalashnikov in the desert.

Johnny looks at me with a newfound sparkle in his eye.

"I guess we're all set then!" he says.

More than you know, my hot English sausage, more than you know.

Chapter Six

Our "quaint" Chiang Mai guesthouse is an asbestos shack with ten mats positioned symmetrically on the dirty floor. Not my first choice, but who wants to be high-maintenance at this juncture? All the mats are vacant save for one, upon which lies a skinny, beige, bald man reading a book, his striking green eyes shooting out like emeralds from his gaunt face as we enter. Hugh's eyes burst through his bullet-proof glasses in reciprocity.

"Hello, friend!" Hugh ejaculates at alarming volume.

"Hallo," the man replies quietly, his smile innocent and genuine. His accent and head shape are a dead giveaway: Israeli. "I'm Gadi."

"I'm Hugh."

"I'm Johnny."

"*Ani Iris*," I say in Hebrew, much to his surprise.

"*Yisraelit?*" he asks, whereupon we instantly engage in the highly popular Israeli "What a small world!" game of "Do you know so and so?/I served with so and so!" with much Hebraic enthusiasm. By our fourteenth mutual friend, I realize Johnny and Hugh have been standing there in total incomprehension like smiling crumpets, so I revert back to English.

"We're leaving on a trek tomorrow, Gadi, do you want to

join us?" I ask, adhering to my *always good to have another Jew around* policy.

"Yes!" Gadi replies, touched by my offer. I sense this man has been waiting for someone to invite him to something for quite some time.

"It's settled then!" Hugh declares. "We leave at the crack of dawn. Better get some sleep!"

Johnny quickly claims a mat at the far end of the room. I eye the one adjacent to his, but Hugh's already moving toward it. Shit. I'm all the way on the other side of the room, I'll never make it in time. With much aggression, I hurl my twenty kilo rucksack toward the prize mat, nearly slicing Hugh's head off in the process. The rucksack lands with a claimful thud, and I prance over in victory as Hugh looks on, confused. Call it discreet urban planning if you will, with a hint of subtlety and nonchalance. My trademark.

2:00 A.M. Sleep is but an impossible dream right now. I'm surrounded by three deviated septums passionately belting out a jazzy tune in three-part harmony. The flesh-eating bugs aren't helping either.

3:30 A.M. Bedbugs are getting feistier. Maybe they like the music. Must get off mat now.

4:45 A.M. I burst into an awkward jig in an attempt to take my mind off the snoring and scratching.

5:00 A.M. The septums have launched into a Louie Prima number. I'm scratching in rhythm in the center of the room, when Johnny stirs unexpectedly. I freeze, leg in the air, fingernails embedded in my left butt cheek.

"Are you all right?" he mumbles dreamily.

"I think I have fleas in my mat."

"Oh shit, I hate that!"

I stand there for a beat, smiling stupidly.

"Would you like to join me in here?" he says, opening his calamined sleeping bag.

"Oh, no, thank you, I'm fine!" I blout, denying myself the very pleasure I've been dreaming of since the moment I laid eyes on him.

Maybe I'm just not ready.

Or maybe I'm just an idiot.

The ass crack of dawn. It's day one of our trek, and there is an anticipatory thrill in the air. Johnny and Hugh have gone off to arrange a guide, leaving Gadi and me to pack up.

"Aren't you excited?!" I ask, energized despite my lack of sleep.

"I'm dying!" he replies.

"Me, too! I can't wait!"

"No really, I'm dying. I have cancer. I just wanted you to know."

"Excuse me?"

His face tells me he's not kidding. At a loss, I say the one thing I know how to say really well.

"I'm sorry."

Gadi looks amused at this answer.

"What are you sorry for? It's not *your* fault!" he says with a laugh.

I can't tell if he's making light of the situation for his sake or mine. Probably both. If only I could get this horrified expression off my face.

A pregnant pause leads to an abortive one. Must say something quick.

"Aren't your parents worried about you traveling like this?"

"Oh, they don't speak to me anymore. When they found out I had cancer, they decided I was a disgrace to the family."

And I thought my parents were problematic.

"After being in chemo for six months, I finally told the doctors no more. I wanted to stop the nausea, gain some strength back, and basically travel until I die. And here I am."

He props a pillow under his bony elbow. "I feel happy," he says genuinely. "I feel alive!"

I nod in support. His story isn't so sad after all!

"I won't be able to feel that much longer. Two months at the most."

Razor anyone?

I finally manage to produce a faint smile. "That's wonderful," I say, knowing full well that the weepy pity in my eyes betrays me. Gadi has nothing to add to my forced display of ebullience, so we just sit there, gawking at the floor, silently contemplating his mortality.

Hugh bursts into the room with an animated stride. Thank God. The man deserves a year's worth of free dental work for this entrance.

"We leave in an hour!" he barks with military flair. "And I told the guide NO tourist bullshit, *ten* hours of walking a day, *back jungle* only."

I glance up at Cancerman to gauge his reaction, hoping he's just as terrified as I am.

Nope. The fucker's glowing with enthusiasm. Hey, what's he got to lose? I'm the one who has to uphold the commando façade I've created for myself.

I guess this is it. I either bite the bullet for the next three days in the "back jungle"—whatever the hell that means—or get left alone in Chiang Mai to my own devices. It's a no-brainer. After hearing Gadi's story, alone is the last thing I want to be.

Chapter Seven

Gadi looks especially scrawny this morning. Must be the enormous Paddington hat he's wearing. I've packed light for our three-day journey, carrying only a bottle of water, change of underwear, and my journal. I'm wearing long pants, a long shirt, and for backup have also lathered on seven layers of antimalarial mosquito repellant. Hugh and Johnny, on the other hand, are equipped for small-scale warfare, toting three canteens, two mag lights, a Bunsen burner, four flares, six bottles of Thai whiskey, one large machete, and a frying pan.

Our guide is a limber Thai boy with long toenails and a sparkle in his eye, whom I've punfully dubbed "Guido." In a clanky jeep we are driven to the foot of a large mountain. Base camp. To be honest, I don't really feel like getting out, it's so comfortable in here, not having to move and all. But it's time. Guido leaps out, Cancerman takes my hand, the Brit Battalion gives the group a confident commencement nod, and we set off.

The ascent into the jungley mountains is very steep, and Johnny, Hugh, and Guido quickly progress ahead. I stagger behind with Gadi, under the guise of "keeping him company."

I've decided to make his final days on the planet fun and festive. So, possessor of great ideas that I am, I suggest playing a game called "It Could Be Worse." The idea is to name all the things that could be happening to you that are worse than dying of cancer. "You start!" Gadi says, up for the challenge. And so we rotate: I do "having no legs," he does "being born blind." The only problem is that we cover everything worse than cancer in about twenty minutes, and by the time we hit "slow burning at the stake while listening to the Smiths," I notice Gadi ain't looking so hot. He can't breathe, he's red as a beet, and his eyes are about to bust out of their sockets. He leans heavily against a tree, clutching his awning. I run ahead to find Guido, whom I'm surprised to find resting on the side of the trail, smoking a very fat cigarette.

By the time we get back to Gadi, he's looking a bit better. Guido suggests we turn back, but Gadi insists we continue, but at a slower pace, please.

"Of course," Guido replies, obviously traumatized by some past ailing-trekker litigation.

The next two hours are taken *at a crawl*. In fact, we're going so slow, I'm beginning to feel sick myself. At this rate we're all going to die of futility and inefficiency, not to mention embarrassment and boredom.

Thank God we've reached the friendly plateau segment of the trail. It's clear by now that Guido has taken charge of the cheering committee, and so I feel guilt-free excusing myself to venture ahead at a quicker pace.

Galloping along the mountain ridge, I quickly gain ground, leaving Gadi and Guido far behind. Now we're talking. I forge ahead with gusto, wrapping around the first mountain and commencing the climb up the next. I'm amazed my heart hasn't given out yet. Maybe I'm in better shape than I thought! (Compared to the stoned and terminally ill, that is.) At this rate, I'll catch up with Hugh and Johnny in no time, and how impressed will they be!

Skip. Trot. Run. Leap. Jesus! How cool am I right now?! Alone in this magnificent landscape, far away from home, pounding the dirt away in trekkie bliss. Just me and the jungle. I am invincible! This is Thailand, this is what I came for! If only that putzfuck Boaz could see me now!

Ooooh. The jungle is getting more and more mysterious. A thickening of the foliage. A thinning of the air. A heavying of my sweat. Crap. My skin's starting to burn. Time for a malaria skin check. Nope, no bites, just some red splotches. Must be the industrial-strength DEET taking effect. Well, better disintegrated skin than malaria, right? Pretty soon the mosquitoes won't have any skin to bite into at all, and that's as good a repellant as any.

I wonder how Gadi is holding up. How selfish of me, leaving him like that with Guido. But it's hard to stay perky when a man is shriveling right before your very eyes. And what's gonna happen after the trek? Are we going to stay together? The last thing I need is to get emotionally attached to someone, only to have them die on me one morning over hash browns and Sprite. What a horrid thought. Horrid and selfish. I can't believe I just thought it. Most people would feel it an honor, a privilege to entertain a poor soul on his last days on earth, but not me. No, I'm a piece of shit. But you know what? I will fight my piece-of-shithoodness. I will embrace Gadi with all my heart.

I'll just do it in spurts.

The heat has gotten unbearable. I'm contemplating stripping down to my bra, but that would reveal unDEETed skin, and we can't have that. If my stupid sweat would just disengage from the T-shirt it has so lovingly glued to my body, it could actually be of some use and cool me down.

Oh look, I've hit yet *another* turn. Whoopee. I can't believe I haven't run into Johnny and Hugh yet. How fast could they be going?! By now the jungle has gotten so thick, I have to manually clear a path with my hands. Mr. Miyagi would be proud. *Swoosh! Swoosh! Swoosh!* I go, tearing through the brush, biceptually revealing my increasing exhaustion. I guess this is what Hugh meant by "back jungle."

I'm not even sure I'm on the right path anymore, especially since there's no path to speak of. Hasn't been one for hours. Maybe I should wait for Gadi and Guido. But where? There's barely any space to sit between the palms and the other jungley plants I can't define. No, all I can do is stand and wait.

So I stand and wait. For about a second, whereupon that trusty feeling of idiocy kicks in. I can't just keep standing here like a moron. Not only is the dynamic duo at least two hours behind me, I don't even know if I'm on the right path. I could be waiting here for nothing. I must keep on.

Ow. I think a chunk of my stomach just fell off. Yep. The decomposing has begun. Fuck malaria and fuck mosquitoes, I need to wash this shmutz off my body. But only a tiny bit of water remains in my canteen. Oh well. Hydration is overrated anyway. Must tend to burning flesh.

Ahhhhhh.

*   *   *

The path is precariously curving around the mountain edge. One wrong step and I'll plummet into the canyon depths, without Kathleen Turner's crotch to pad my fall.

I slowly turn the corner. The air temperature drops sharply. It dawns on me that the sun is setting. I've been walking alone all day. I am officially lost. Shit.

I force myself to pick up the pace again, not even bothering to move the branches aside, just thwacking my face into them. Faster and faster I run, in a ridiculous effort to catch up with the Brit Brigade before dark. My legs are swollen. My face is burning and bleeding with sweat and scratches. My stomach is numb and my eyes are beginning to lose focus.

Finally, a clearing! The view is breathtaking. Literally— I can't fucking breathe. A vast canyon stretches before me. And all the way across the canyon a majestic mountain looms. And on that majestic mountain, two dots are in motion. The dots are Johnny and Hugh. They're on a completely different mountain. How the FUCK did they get on a COMPLETELY DIFFERENT MOUNTAIN?

Shit shit shit. I'm worse off track than I thought. And the sun is setting like a motherfucker. Plodding faster toward nowhere is pointless. It's time for more drastic measures, like screaming for help.

Wait. I can't just scream for help like a panicking idiot— what if someone hears me? No, I must keep it light and festive, melodic, with a playful air.

"He-LL-oOoO!!!"

Silence. Not even an echo for good measure. Fuck festive.

"HEEEEELLLLLLP!!!"

"HELLO!!!"

"HELP!!!!"

"HEEEEEEEEEEEEEEELP!!"

Nothing. And with an exasperated sigh, the sun bids me adieu.

Within minutes it has gone completely dark. The moon apparently has better things to do tonight than show up. Cocky bastard. I have no choice—I must wait till they find me. *If* they find me.

Good God. I could spend the whole night in this stupid shithole of back jungle.

I manage to clear a small patch on the ground and take a seat. For the first time in many hours, my body is truly still. And tired. All it can do now is wait.

Unbelievable. I'm traveling with a terminal cancer patient, and yet *I'm* the one on the death trek.

It's so dark, I can't even feel my own presence. I rummage through my bag and take out my underwear. I sniff it deeply, finding comfort in the familiar smell of Ima's fabric softener. Poor Ima. She still thinks I'm on an organized temple tour with Boaz. Does she really deserve to hear that her daughter found her untimely demise in the back jungles of Thailand? Wasn't my brother's plight enough?

Chapter Eight

Still here. I have no idea how long it's been. Fascinating how time takes on a different quality when external stimuli are nonexistent.

I'm beginning to wonder if I really am going to be abandoned here. It could happen. It wouldn't be the first time I was abandoned. Oh, cut the pity parade, woman. Plenty of people have died in the jungle who have never been abandoned before, so don't make yourself all "par for the course victimized" and shit.

Pitpitpitpitpitpitpit.

What the hell was that?

Pitpitpitpitpitpitpit.

Something's scurrying in the bushes. An animal? I forgot about them. The animals.

"Hello?" I call out, hoping the animals speak English.

PITPITPITPITPITIPITPIT.

"Hello!"

PITPITPITPITPITPITPITPITPIT.

Jesus Christ, it's getting closer. Definitely footsteps. Too fast to be human though. Maybe it's a midget. Whatever it is, it just spit. Animals don't spit, do they? God help me, I can't see a fucking thing.

"Hello?"

Another spit. Definitely human. More scampering. It seems to be circling me or something.

Pitpitpitpitpitpitpit.

"Okay, that's enough! Don't tease me like that, you midget alien fuck! If you're here to do some business, then get it over with!"

It stops. It's so dark, for all I know it could be standing right in front of me.

Click.

A beam of flashlight. That illuminates the most disturbing flat-faced pockmarked red-toothed Thai man this world has ever seen. And by all Nordic standards, a midget.

I find myself paralyzed. Fear? Disgust? Who cares. I can't move.

He offers me his hand. I'm not quite sure if it's the hand that'll lead me to slaughter, but it's not like I'm about to wait around for the handsome nice brother to show up.

Wow. His skin's surprisingly soft. I must remember to ask him what lotion he uses before he rapes and pillages me.

Midgetmaster leads me farther up the mountain. Neither of us is really attempting small talk. It's better this way, I think—my mind has peace to wander off into that terrifying place known as reality.

I squeeze my captor's hand in an ironic attempt to gain comfort from the very source of my anxiety. He squeezes back. His thumb caresses mine. Easy there, Pizzaface. Just cuz I was chilling in the jungle for no reason doesn't mean I'm a whore, you know!

We enter a heavily wooded area, the air warmer yet much

darker and more ominous than the already pitch black it was a moment ago.

I'm fully aware of how these kidnapping things work. First a ransom call, then negotiations (if I'm lucky). At some point Syria or Iran become involved, citing Israel's occupation as the reason behind the kidnapping. It's all very simple.

Aha. We've reached the peak. At the bottom of the mountain several small huts await. I take a deep breath, and with a final hand-squeeze, we gallop downhill at an alarming speed, the stalks of palm pelting our faces as we go, like an S&M couples workshop gone awry.

The trio of huts stare back at me ominously. I must say the streets are pretty quiet for a death village. No eager mobs or visible nooses. That's a good sign. Pizzaface drags my exhausted body toward the central hut. I really wish he wouldn't dig his nails into my palm like that—it's bad form.

There is mumbling from within. Sounds like a big group inside. I guess this is where it all goes down. PF is standing behind me, clearly waiting for me to open the door. Some gentleman. I should've known, considering his decorumless conduct the entire evening thus far. With a deep stuttered breath, I push the hut flap open with false bravado, unsure of what awaits.

A bonfire.

And sitting there . . . holding a massive coconut bong . . . is none other than . . . Johnny.

Gadi and Hugh are right there next to him, eating coconut soup from an identical receptacle. They all nod nonchalantly at my entrance, as if I were right on schedule. Thanks for the hugs of comfort guys—really, don't get up, I'm fine.

Holding back my tears, I quietly join the circle, nervously contemplating the two coconut delights in circulation.

Both terrify me. With good reason. I didn't go to high school in the U.S., hence I was not privy to the standard American practice of trying every un/controlled substance by ninth grade. No, in Israel, at Herzelia High, pot was tantamount taboo to crack. The biggest news senior year was that Rina got an abortion and Nati got caught smoking Marlboros behind the gym.

Then, of course, there's also my brother, fifteen years older than me and severely mentally handicapped. After all these years, you'd think the family would've made peace with his predicament, or at least adjusted to it, but we're far from it, each member of the family with his or her own dysfunctional coping mechanisms, or lack thereof. I choke up every time I go visit him, which isn't as often as I know I should. My mother sleeps with her feet hanging off the bed just in case she needs to jump out and tend to my brother in the middle of the night, despite the fact that he has not lived at home in over twenty years. My father is haunted by the notion that "it's his fault." Back when my brother's mental retardation first revealed itself, my parents were a young couple living in Israel, desperately doing everything they could to assess his condition, including some tests (that I guess were new at the time, or at least involved some spinal tapping, I'm not quite sure). It is after those tests that my father claims my brother stopped singing. "He used to sing," my father keeps saying, "and then after those tests he stopped, he stopped singing." I've sadly found that trying to make my father believe otherwise is pointless, and he continues to punish himself and contemplate these horrible scenarios.

I wish there were a way to love my brother without so much pain involved. To love him without the dagger of helplessness looming over us at all times. I don't know if other families "cope" better, and to be honest it doesn't really matter; the tragedy of my brother scorches my family's heart on a daily basis.

After all that, how could I even fathom taking my healthy brain for granted and risk damaging it with harmful substances? I could never disrespect you like that my sweet brother. Never.

I did, however, just spend several hours lost in the jungle and am ready for my first bong hit. Please forgive me.

I snatch the evil coconut out of Hugh's hands and suck so hard even Pizzaface is taken aback. There's hope for me yet.

Throop. BubblebubblePhwoooooooCoughCoughHack-HackAhhhhhh.

My virgin brain welcomes the giddy greenery with open neurons. Within seconds I'm giggling maniacally. I'm laughing so hard, I start laughing nervously at my laughter, anxiously searching the immediate environment for some amusing stimuli to justify this bout of hysteria. My eyes meet Johnny's g(l)aze. His grin is all the comfort I need, and I immediately forgive his indifference at my traumatic jungle escapade.

Come to think of it, tonight would be the perfect night to stage my sexual assault—Johnny's too baked to notice how inexperienced I am, and I'm giddy enough to let King Kong take a private tour!

With a sudden burst of energy, I leap up from the stoner circle, rush to the sleeping quarters, strip down to my underwear and tank top, and lay by Johnny's mat, angling myself in the most enticing position possible: left leg over right, midriff fully exposed.

I lay in this position for quite a while. Finally, through semiclosed feigned sleep-eye, I see Johnny stagger into the hut. He eyes me briefly, then stumbles outside to brush his teeth (without water, a technique he swears saved him in India).

Upon returning, he finds me in enticing position B: on my side, right leg over left, giving my buttock and thigh just the right line—voluptuous, but not flabby.

I can feel his eyes slowly trace my body.

"You awake?" he whispers.

His voice coats my body like honey. I want to respond, but my mouth won't move. Johnny tumbles into his sleeping bag and turns away. Dammit, woman, do something! I release a sexy "I'm only half asleep" moan and enter position C: the open-legged "I'm a sleeping whore" pose.

It works! He turns back around. The touch of his breath on my face zaps my eyes open, and for a moment we stare intensely at each other. He silently unzips his sleeping bag. This time I crawl in, my heart beating so hard the mat gyrates back and forth from its palpitations.

I lay down next to him, stiff as a corpse. What if he makes a move—what do I do then? Do I tell him I'm a virgin? Pretend I want to take it slow? I don't even know how to give a decent hand job!

He leans over and kisses me. A soft coconut marijuana kiss. I can feel his majestic member up against me. Won't be long before he busts it out. Must decide now: Am I ready for the pain? The penetration? The humiliation?

His underwear's off. Oh boy. I jolt up and rush back to my virginal cocoon, clutching my stomach, praying for narcolepsy.

"Take your time," he velvets knowingly. "I can wait."

His compassion only makes my inadequacy more painful. As does the papal kiss he promptly delivers to my forehead a second before instantaneously descending into a stoned slumber.

I, on the other hand, remain awake all night, staring at his flaring nostrils, "accidentally" nudging his body every twenty minutes, hoping he'll awaken and find his penis inexorably heading toward my vagina. No such luck. I end up spending the whole night sporadically kicking his baked corpse in vain, quietly self-stimulating myself in desperation.

So much for a "just got lost in the jungle" pity fuck.

Chapter Nine

My nocturnal dread over facing Johnny this morning has proven to be for naught. The man has been so sweet to me all day that I'm beginning to wonder if he even remembers what happened last night. Maybe he thinks we shtooped like rabbits. Considering he hasn't left my side since we reentered the jungle, I must have been pretty good. Not only has he been holding my hand and helping me through the tough patches, he's also been making sure we walk at a pace everyone can tolerate. The man is a saint. A hot saint.

Everyone is in great spirits, especially Guido, who won't shut up about some wonderful "surprise" at lunchtime. Turns out he's not full of shit. After a pleasantly gradual ascent, we arrive at the most stunning waterfall I've ever seen.

Within seconds Gadi is in the water splashing like a recently released inmate. He is the happiest man alive. His smile is so deep I want to cry. Instead, I strip down to underwear and bra, jump in, and waddle his way. Without warning, I hug him with so much love that we're both taken aback. I don't think anyone has hugged Gadi for a long, long time. We're trembling, pent-up emotes pulsing through our bodies—feet to legs to rib cage to throat, stopping just short of creating our own teary little waterfall.

Our floodful unity is broken by a tap on my shoulder.

I turn around to find Johnny in his tightey maroonies. He grabs me and throws me high in the air. I land with a messy splash and am just about to come up for air when I spot Johnny's immersed privates before me. His bulge is massive. MASSIVE. How the hell do I find these guys?

I shoot out of the water and leap onto Johnny's firm body like a leech, taking advantage of this playful excuse for skin-to-skin contact. He lets out a startled yelp, and we commence a frenzied water fight. He tosses me to and fro; I grab his huge cock and swing him around.

Just kidding.

With much exhaustion and arousal we join the others, who are lizardly basking in the sun. This whole water fight thing has given me new sexual confidence.

"You want a massage, Johnny?"

He turns to Hugh. I fear a mocking coming on.

"How can I say no to a beautiful Israeli woman, Hugh?"

"I don't know, my friend . . . I guess you can't."

God save the queen.

"Do you want me to come over there, Iris, or you come over here?"

I'm about to come all over the place, my sweet.

"You stay right there, Johnny, I'll be right over."

Johnny flips on to his stomach like a good boy. I plop sloppily onto his damp rear end, and for the next half hour give him the back rub of a lifetime. This I can do. This I can handle. It's once I get him going that I'm worried about.

We're back at the good ole asbestos shack in Chiang Mai. Just me, Johnny, and Hugh. Gadi has just left for India. I thought I'd be relieved, but I'm not. I was very sad to see him go. In a few months he'll no longer be among the living. But I must focus on his ability to make the most of what's left of his life. I must focus on his determination, his joy. He's obviously better at that than I am, that's for sure. I'm just a coward. I live in fear of hurt and disappointment at every turn. Like now, for instance, when it just dawned on me that my allotted time with Johnny is up. The offer was to travel together for a few days, and those few days are over. At any moment he and Hugh could give me the ole farewell talk, and that petrifies me. The fact that I've fallen in love with Johnny is not helping matters either.

I've been doing my best to hide my anxiety, chirping around the room, reorganizing the mats in various geometric configurations.

"I'm knackered," Johnny declares. "I'm going to take a nap."

Hugh concurs, and within seconds they're snoring their heads off. Remarkable. How do these guys just jump into different states of consciousness with such ease? My mind has to go through four levels of obsessive neuroses first.

Lying next to Johnny's head, as always, is his journal. A small, black, leather-bound book. He writes in it every chance he gets. I'm sure he writes about me, too. He must. I wonder what he writes. It's sitting right there. His journal. *His journal.* You can't get any more private than that. I couldn't possibly look through it. Could I? No. I couldn't. Well, maybe just a page. Just to ease my anxiety, you know, see how he feels. For my peace of mind. For my health. For my sanity. I deserve that much, after all I've been through.

Johnny and Hugh's septums launch into a fresh rendition

of "Summertime." I find the duet orchestration slightly menacing. I crawl over toward the journal. Quietly. This is by far the most unethical thing I've ever done. At least I'm doing it to music. Easy . . . easy . . . breathe . . . Pick it up, slowly . . . *slowly, dammit* . . . Ew . . . I feel dirty just touching it . . . Oh look, his pen's inside . . . I'll just open it to that page. If it happens to say something about me, then great; if not, it's my loss, and I'll put the journal back and never touch it again. That's the deal, take it or leave it.

Damn his handwriting is small. I can barely make it out. Okay, one line. One line only.

Something something . . . *are small but nicely formed something* . . .

Hmm. He better be referring to my breasts. Sweet. There's gotta be more. One more line. Just one more line.

She obviously likes me—gave me massage at waterfall etc.

"Etc.?" Who the hell writes "etc." in their personal journal?! What does that mean? Such ambiguous noninformative writing, it's horrible.

Want something . . . *private time with Hugh*.

I knew it. They can't wait to get rid of me. I'm going to cry. Yes. A tear has made an appearance. It must've been a loud one, because Johnny awakens. My, how life repeats itself.

"What's wrong?" he asks. My darling is so perceptive. I hope I don't have NONETHICAL SCUM written on my forehead, because that's how I feel.

"I'm . . . just sad that Gadi's gone."

"Yes, he's a sweet bloke, isn't he."

I'm shivering. I've known this man five days, and just the thought of him leaving me is making me shake. He senses something deeper and once again invites me into his cocoon of love. Like a child scared of the dark, I crawl in needily and close my eyes, unable to handle eye contact.

"We have a big travel day tomorrow," he whispers offhandedly.

"Where are you going?" I sputter.

"You mean, where are *we* going?"

The teardrop sneaks out from under my closed eyelid. Johnny wipes it gently with his finger.

"We're heading up to Chiang Rai on motorbikes," he whispers. "You *are* coming, are you not? We couldn't possibly part with you so soon."

The tear stops by my left nostril.

"Yes, yes I'd like to come . . . that is, if it's not a burden."

"Don't be silly, Iris. You are delightful."

Did you hear that? I am delightful. *Delightful!* Who knew?

"Thanks, Johnny."

He leans in for a kiss. It is long and tender and magnificent. And once it's completed, he quietly falls asleep in my arms.

I am in heaven.

Chapter Ten

Our second day in Chiang Rai and it's safe to say that Johnny and I are officially a couple. A couple in all respects but one. But fret not. Now that I'm openly in love with the man, I'm ready to make love. I've grown. I've matured. I'm hornier. Oh, and I'm in love. Did I fail to mention that I'm *in love*?

A very romantic dinner is currently in progress. It's just me, Johnny, and Hugh. Hugh is turning out to be a third-wheel fetishist of sorts, but at the same time I do feel sorry for him; after all he is still single, the least we can do is keep him company. Luckily, Johnny was smart enough to select a two-room suite at the guesthouse. I guess Hugh will just have to buy earplugs! Heh heh.

My leg is caressing Johnny's thigh under the table. I think I just hit his nut. Good. Get acquainted, young lady, that way you won't be so freaked out later tonight. Ooh. Just touched it again. Nudge it. Easy. Easy. I look up, expecting some sort of smirk of pleasure or at least an acknowledgment that I'm in contact with his left testicle, but Johnny's not even looking at me. Something over my shoulder has obviously caught his attention. Hugh, too, is distracted.

"What the hell is the big attraction?" I say turning around.

Aha. A sizzling Thai woman is sipping a beverage at the bar.

"She's obviously a hooker," I say, not attempting to hide my disgust.

"She's bloody gorgeous," Johnny replies, extricating his leg from my entrenched claw and approaching her at the bar with mucho swagger. My jaw bungees to the ground.

Within seconds the bitch is giggling at a joke he hasn't even made yet. I watch, horrified, as she touches his shoulder, giggling louder and louder. He's fucking hilarious, isn't he? Nausea bubbles greenly in my throat. Look away, I tell myself, but I can't. *What masochistic eyes you have, Iris. Better to view the ongoing seduction with, my sweet!*

Her hand just got promoted to rubbing his crotch. What a disgrace. In the middle of the bloody restaurant! Do you have no shame, woman? That's where *my* hand's supposed to be!

This is getting torturous. I'm better than this. My dignity must be preserved. I know what I must do. I must head back to the guesthouse, put on some sexy underwear, and prep a scalding admonition speech for Johnny upon his return.

> *Lights up.*
> *Iris, dressed in a tasteful nightie, is pacing on the bed. It has been four hours since Johnny began his sketchy interaction with the disgusting prostitute. In the interim, Iris has perfected a scalding admonition speech, which she delivers to a small ant napping in the corner of the room.*

Johnny sure is giving me plenty of time to rehearse. I've run the damn speech so many times, it has lost its scalding admonitional quality. I sound more like an ethics professor than a pissed-off girlfriend. The fact is, he's not coming back for a while. He's probably plastered at the bar, too drunk to walk back home.

I'm tired of pacing. I know! I'll sleep sprawled across the bed in extended T formation in protest. That'll show him.

An hour later I'm abruptly awakened, not by the septum stylings of Miles Davis, but by Johnny's copulatory howling in the other room.

Unh.

Unh.

Unh.

Oh!

Bloody hell.

Yes!

Oh Johnny! JOHNEEE!

Yes! Yes!

With every groan of pleasure, my heart carves out another chunk of my stomach. By their third orgasm, a complete ulcer has formed.

Make it stop.

Please.

Chapter Eleven

The fuckers didn't stop all night. In fact, they only went mute about five minutes ago.

I've been wondering who'll be the first to venture into my room to use the bathroom. It's her.

"Hallo!" she says to me with a smile. I can't help but smile back. Damn social conditioning. Slutsky disappears into the bathroom, and I take a deep breath as the shower begins to cleanse her Johnnied body. Hmmm. Maybe this isn't so bad. Maybe I can handle this. Johnny follows her in with a towel wrapped around his waist. There is no way I can handle this.

My ears continue their masochistic endeavors regardless, straining for the sounds of activity from under the jet stream. All I pick up are mumblings in broken English. Wait. No. That's not broken English. Those are the sounds of tears. Yes, she's crying. Sobbing actually. Johnny must have just told her he's in love with me, and that she was only a temporary release from his sexual abstinence. I knew it! Sorry, honey, that's the way it has to be. Jewish girl wins out over Thai whore. Happens all the time.

Whoa. Bitch be yelling now. Maybe she'll slap him. Slap him! He deserves it! If I weren't hiding under the sheets right now, I'd do it myself! Some ruffling sounds. A zipper. She storms out of the shower and out the door, the sound of fading stilettos punctuating her departure. Johnny remains on the other side of the curtain, still under the jet stream. For a long time. What could he be cleaning in there?

I have no idea what to expect upon his reentry. I've decided to play the understanding card; I figure if I'm too pissed off, I'll scare him away—pseudo-virgins have only a limited supply of tolerable bitterness. The way I see it, the man had needs and I wasn't meeting them. Yes, he could have exhibited more tact, i.e., not fucked someone in the next room—but maybe her apartment was unsuitable for a blue-ball releasecapade.

The water stops. I swiftly fix my hair. Johnny steps out looking like a Paco Rabanne ad.

"Good morning, Little Iris!" he says, shooting me an invigorated wink.

"Good morning," I reply icily. The bitter bunny is slowly emerging, and I can't do anything to stop it.

"Not feeling well?" he asks.

Are men that dumb? They can't be. They just can't.

"No, Johnny, I feel *fine*. I just didn't get much sleep last night . . . what with the really *loud sex* and all."

A clumsy pause tumbles into the air, struggling to dissipate into word form.

"I'm sorry, luv," he coos, sitting on the bed, tenderly taking my hand. "You understand, don't you?"

Butter am I.

"Yes, Johnny."

"Good, I'm glad," he says, kissing my hand with a smile.

I smile back.

I always do.

By the way, I'm not being a pathetic doormat. I'm simply being loving and understanding. That's what relationships are all about. Mistakes and forgiveness. He makes them and I forgive them. Look, I'm no angel either. I've been with the guy over a week and have not even remotely satisfied his sexual needs. And have I heard even one complaint? No. Not one. Then again he's been napping for the past three hours. Poor guy is e/motionally exhausted.

Hugh, on the other hand, is perky as can be, and has inexplicably made us some tea. We sip it together on the porch, Johnny's tractorshnoz echoing in the background.

"You're in love, girl." Hugh whispers.

"Yes, I guess I am."

"Well, I hate to say this, but get used to it," he states with strange satisfaction.

"I will." How can one not get used to being in love?

"The man is a master, you know," he says, a gleam of admiration in his eye. "He never has to pay for it."

"Excuse me?"

"These girls just fall at his feet. I don't know how he does it."

I don't like where this conversation is heading.

"Me?" he continues animatedly. "If I don't show them fifty baht, they won't even let me buy them a drink, let alone a shag, but not Mr. Wade—no, not Johnny Wade. He gets them every time, dozens and dozens of gorgeous women, all for free. He's never paid, not even once. I remember this one time in Kuala Lumpur—"

"Okay, Hugh! I got it! *Not even once.* That's great. That's fucking great."

My harsh glare pierces a hole through his shot glasses. He rubs his eyes from the burn.

Doesn't Hugh get it?! Last night was a onetime thing. A onetime thing.

"I don't care about his past, Hugh, he's changed. He's found *me,* you see."

"Maybe you're right. He does seem to really like you, Iris. More than any other woman we've met on this trip."

That's more like it. I pour Hugh some more tea, and we return to our quiet sipping at sunset. I'm glad he's seen the light.

"And trust me, Iris, we've met a lot of women on this trip. A *lot!*"

God I hope the tea burns his lip.

Less than twenty-four hours after the onetime thing, I am introduced to pro bono prostitute number two.

> *Welcome, PBP #2, and thank you for shattering our hopes for anomaly. We hope your stay at Casa Free Fuck will be to your liking. Out of respect for the sad lump lying in the adjacent room, please keep the groaning down to a minimum. Thank you.*
>
> *The Management.*

And the PBPs just keep on coming! Who knew there were so many philanthropic souls available on a nightly basis? All with tryst-unsuitable apartments, too!

The pattern is consistent: Johnny seeks the girls out at various locales—the restaurant, bar, neighborhood strip club. He finds "a lady" to his liking, strolls over her way, makes about four jokes before she gives him a crotch rub, and then brings her back to the guesthouse. They fuck. She enters the shower. He follows. He says something to her, she throws a fit and storms off. Hugh turns to me and makes some comment à la "Unbelievable, the man's a master" or "Brilliant."

To be perfectly honest, I, too, have developed an amazement at Johnny's freebiebility.

"How does he do it, Hugh?"

Hugh goes into Hercule Poirot mode, embarking on a careful breakdown of Johnny's technique.

"Promises are made," he says. "Marriage. Papers. A life in London. A house in Cornwall."

"I see. And the next morning when they're both sudsing each other's butt cheeks, he tells them it's not gonna happen."

"Not exactly. He tells them he's off to India and will be back in Chiang Rai in three months' time."

"And they believe him?"

"I guess. What difference does it make? They're prostitutes!"

Prostitutes, yes. But they're also women who see Johnny as salvation from their predicament. I can relate. I don't know what's more repulsive—his behavior, or the fact that it has had absolutely no detrimental effect on my love for the man. On the contrary, it only makes me want him more. In the boxing ring of my heart, the man's charm seems to have utterly knocked out his vice. I mean we must've hit pro bono #5 by now and I'm *still* hanging around. What's left of me, that is. That sweet, witty Israeli girl who Johnny was initially charmed by has turned into a pouty, joyless, self-pitying clump of kaka. The cursed demon bittermope has taken over. Nobody wants to hang around me anymore. Myself included.

Maybe instead of bitching and sulking, I should do something useful. Like pick up parting gifts for the girls, or provide them with a cup of coffee for the road. Maybe if I did that, Johnny would recognize what a remarkably kind, supportive, low-maintenance soul I am, forget about these meaningless one-nighters, and come crawling back to me!

And so I do. But it doesn't take long before I run out of creative gift ideas and realize the Thai are not big coffee drinkers. All is not lost, however. Tonight I'm gonna give it one last shot. Tonight I'm gonna really show my support. Tonight—I'm tagging along.

Chapter Twelve

Just your average suburban strip joint, no airborne fruit or anything of that ilk. Simply a glossy stage surrounded by barstools, a few tables, and a handful of ladies working the poles.

One woman is particularly stunning; legs that go on for miles, long silky black hair, flexible spine. She's not like the other girls. Her dancing has a smoother, more mature quality to it, as if Pina Bausch were involved in the initial choreography process. Her features are more pronounced than her flatter-faced colleagues, her presence intensely overpowering. Johnny can't take his eyes off her. Neither can I.

With a nod she approaches. I zestfully elbow Johnny in a "Good choice, my man!" kind of way. He's pleasantly surprised by my atta-boy attitude, and for the first time in days, he looks me straight in the eye, giving me a comradey thumbs up.

I keep whooping away as she de-stages and commences a hard-core grind on his lap. Up and down she goes. Oh! What fun is being had by all!

"Oh yeah!" I yell, shooting another elbow out Johnny's way, only this time jabbing the girl's rib cage by accident.

"Oops," I squeak sheepishly. "Sorry about that."

They both give me an annoyed look before resuming the merry-go-round. I slump over to a stool farther down the stage to prevent any additional mishaps. At least from over here I can watch the action without a fake smile pasted on my face.

Perfecta slows down her dance and looks my way again. What did I do now? I bend down to tie the shoelaces on my flip-flops. When I come back up, she's still looking at me. In fact, she's so focused on looking at me that her turbo grind has slowed down to a dough knead. Johnny's getting confused. As am I. He anxiously tries to steer her attention back to his forgotten shlong, but at this point she's just standing there, staring at me. Great, now Johnny's really going to hate me. Her stare is possessed. She's like a locked sniper. What in God's name is her problem? One accidental rib jab and she won't let me forget it! Oh crap, now she's getting up. Perfect. I've ruined everything. Johnny is shocked— a woman willingly disembarking from his carnival crotch? Unprecedented!

She walks my way, pedestrian-like, as if approaching the checkout counter at Walgreens, yeast infection ointment in hand. She takes a seat.

"How old are you?" she asks me in well-enunciated English.

"Twenty."

"I have a daughter like you."

"Excuse me?"

"She is eighteen. Student."

The woman sitting before me doesn't look a day over twenty-five.

"*You* have an eighteen-year-old daughter?"

"Yes, yes, I am forty-two."

"Wow."

I can only imagine what *her* daughter's feelings of inadequacy are like, what with a sexy mom that works the laps of drunken foreigners on weeknights. Not to mention her extensive thong collection.

What if Perfecta had been my mother? Would I have grown up to be some spirited tigress instead of this prison cell of amorphous hormonal confusion? My mom's weeknights were mostly spent at home, especially once dad moved out of the house and into Manhattan. Depressing as that may have been, it did save me from the creepy babysitter who made horrible omelets and reveled in washing my mouth out with soap. As if someone had told her that taking archaic sayings literally was okay.

Very soon after Dad moved out, he asked me if I wanted to come see his new apartment one weekend. I did not. I much preferred to sit with him through three hours of Falstaff at the Metropolitan Opera and engage in other such distracting artsy activities during our precious time together, than take a pee in his bathroom and find his girlfriend's toothbrush staring back at me.

I never met the woman, never even saw a photo. I always imagined her to be a mustached, tube-topped, tight-jeaned slut. I'm not sure if that particular image made her existence less upsetting to me or more. It's kind of like putting down ex-boyfriends—it makes you feel good about yourself, but also says something about your horrible taste.

"He your friend?" Perfecta asks, pointing to Johnny, who's still staring at our exchange in disbelief.

"Uh, yes . . . my friend. I guess."

"You like him very much?"

"Yes. I do."

"I understand."

Her face bursts into a warm, maternal smile. She tells me she sensed my feelings for Johnny the minute we entered the club which is why she decided to stop her dance midway. What an act of female chivalry. Truly. I had forgotten such gestures between women were possible. And not just any woman. A professional hooker whose beauty and sensuality are somehow providing me with comfort and inspiration, not feelings of inadequacy and resentment.

She asks me where I'm from and how long I've been traveling. We engage in a lengthy animated discussion about everything from my time in the military to her daughter's school work, all while Johnny and Hugh gawk on. In the course of our conversation, she exhibits an extensive knowledge of spoken Hebrew in its proper syntax, which I can only attribute to a healthy Israeli client list. No surprises there.

I ask her if she'd ever consider sleeping with Johnny for free, in exchange for a "life in England." She laughs heartily, having stopped believing such bullshit twenty years ago.

"Look who comes," she says.

Johnny's approaching slowly. He looks different; his shoulders are a bit hunched, his gait hesitant. I can't believe it, he's actually *intimidated* by her, just because she didn't want him! If only I were on her side of the rejection skill fence. I had best learn some ice-queen skills soon if I want Johnny plodding in my direction that way.

Eyes still to the ground, Johnny mumbles in a low voice, barely audible over the pounding music.

"You ready to go, Iris?"

I act annoyed at the disturbance.

"Are you guys ready to head back? Already?"

"Yeah, we're knackered."

My mentor nudges me under the table.

"Not quite yet, Johnny. A few more minutes, if you don't mind."

"Oh. Okay. We'll be outside."

"Make them wait." She tells me, which I do, for over half an hour, before giving my new best friend a kiss good-bye and exiting the club triumphantly. I find the boys sitting sullenly on a bench outside, devastated by tonight's failures. I, however, am glowing. I'm confident Johnny will see me in a new light after tonight's sultry encounter with Dancing Queen. Hell, *I* see me in a new light.

Seeing Johnny's beautiful face nestled in the pillow beside me is gratifying beyond reason. Though I refrained from making a move on him last night (the last thing I want is our first real night together clouded by another woman's rejection), I do go in for a gentle good-morning kiss.

"Good morning, luv," he mumbles to me sweetly, when Hugh bursts in on our peaceful haven.

"Time to pack," Hugh declares with unprecedented zest. "We're leaving!"

Johnny buries his head under the pillow with a groan.

"Where are we going?" I ask.

"The jungle."

Did I hear correctly?

"What are you talking about, 'the jungle'? We just got *back* from the jungle! I almost got *killed* in the jungle!"

"Yeah, but this is different. We're going to a place off the beaten path."

"Where the fuck were we last week—Detroit?"

"Johnny and I have something we want to try there."

"What? Bungee jumping? Elephant trekking?"

"Opium."

Not the answer I was expecting. And a couple of steps up on my drug-phobia ladder.

"Can't you just get opium at the deli or something?"

"No. We're going to the source. The processors. The best of the best. They're in a highly volatile area, a very secret location, due to the police crackdowns and all. But we found a way in."

This drug talk is making me very nervous.

"Will there be prostitutes there?" I ask.

"No."

"I'm in."

Chapter Thirteen

When I think "remote drug village," I think little Edward James Olmoses scurrying about, animatedly grinding tiny drug pellets. But the opium growers who greet us upon our arrival are far from sketchy back-alley sleazoids with an attitude problem. They are, in actuality, half-naked tribesmen in full indigenous regalia, nifty accessories included.

It seems this entire village is inhabited by members of the Akha tribe. You'd think their *National Geographic*ky presentation was for our sake. But on the contrary; foreigners are not greeted here with dollar photo-ops, but with uneasy suspicion. Meaning this whole tribal thing is the real deal. Authentic Thailand. Finally. And I would've never gotten to see it if it hadn't been for Hugh and Johnny's hunger for highs. Thank you, O' glorious narcotic industry.

After a brief banana pancake lunch, we three are led to a small, dark, hutlike structure on stilts. The chief's already inside, in full opium-prep mode, mixing it with aspirin and mashing it into a paste. He instructs Johnny and Hugh to recline, holds the long pipe up to their mouths, and the smoking begins. Their transphysiomation is a striking vision to behold, a bizarre biological process witnessed in real time. I watch as their flesh gets heavier and heavier with every puff, virtually grafting itself onto the thin mattress beneath them.

Their mind-numbing marathon continues for hours, long after the chief suggests they take a break. Long after he shuffles back to his hut shaking his head. And then for a little while longer. Through my secondhand stupor I can finally see the sun rising. At last Johnny and Hugh put the pipe to rest, physically incapable of lifting it up to their mouths.

There is only so much fun involved in observing heavy drug users in action. A week has been more than enough, and I've finally concluded that Johnny is way too stoned to work on our ailing relationship. It may be time to meet the people that make up this processing powerhouse. It's *Akha time!*

Looks like the hut next door is hosting social night: The entire tribe is sitting in a circle on the front porch. I gawkily join them, grinning stupidly as they ramble on in their tribespeak.

"Stickball, anyone?" I joke with a goofy smile.

It's obvious these people are neither fascinated nor annoyed by my presence. Evidently the whole "I smile at you, then you smile back" ritual has not reached these parts of the world. It's an odd feeling, this lack of reciprocity, to openly spread smiley goodwill and encounter Stonehenge.

Wait. I take that back. There is one smiler sitting in the corner. A rebel. A woman. Looks like the oldest of the bunch (they all look about 104, so it's hard to tell). She's got earlobes the size of soup bowls, but no massive earrings to justify this abnormality. She waves at me and disappears into the hut. A moment later she emerges, heading my way with a large, worn, black book.

She hands it to me, and like magic, the whole group pricks to attention.

Phonetic Akha-English Dictionary

Apparently this "dictionary" was compiled by some anthropologist in the forties. It spells out Akha phrases in phonetic English. The introduction informs me that the Akha tribe enjoy speaking in riddles. That would explain why instead of such useful expressions as "Hello there, could you please pass the opium pipe?" I encounter pages upon pages of more pertinent phrases such as "How many chickens on rooftop mean bad luck?"

I'm contemplating an especially fascinating riddle series involving mudcocks, when it dawns on me that the group has gone completely silent. They are waiting for me. They want me to bust out some riddles for them. In Akha.

So I do. And remarkably, they understand me! Yes, thanks to my skilled pronunciation and exuberant thespianism, I'm able to provide my Akhan brothers and sisters with hours of entertainment. I'm even commended on my comedic timing. I think.

I am the Red Buttons of the Thai Poconos, and it feels grand.

The last time I felt this socially useful was at summer camp ten years ago. I was hiking though the woods with my bunk or group or whatever we called ourselves, whereupon our counselor stepped on a beehive, sending the entire swarm into full attack mode. All the other girls ran for their lives, but for some reason, the second I started to jet, the counselor yelled at me to "Stop!" adding that "They'll get angry if you move!" I obediently froze, crucifixion-like, as every single bee stung my confused body until the entire hive lay dead at my feet.

I didn't cry, though. I even put on a happy face, which was almost impossible considering the nightmare I had just undergone, but the gratitude from the group was worth it. They kept saying I was their hero (well everyone except that one girl who only got one sting but inflated like a blowfish and was rushed to the hospital). I smiled bravely, reveling in the waves of their love and awe at my martyr-dom before boarding the bus home.

When the bus pulled up at my stop on the corner of 246th St., I got out and began to vomit, my body ejecting the massive amount of bee poison in my system in gagging fits and spasms. The nice old lady who feeds the stray cats happened to be nearby. She approached me, put her hand on my back gently, and said:

"Go puke on your own property."

Speaking of which, Johnny and Hugh have not budged in over a week, save to puke and shit. They couldn't be hav-ing a better time. Ah . . . the old addiction-entertainment paradox: too stoned to really enjoy anything, but stoned enough to enjoy everything. I, on the other hand, utterly nonstoned, have been bored out of my mind. Once the rid-dling Akhaite outlet was exhausted, I was back at the drug hut staring at the smack superstars.

The conclusion is inevitable: I need to get back to civi-lization, if nothing else but to call my mother, who is no doubt on the verge of angst arrest, having not heard from me in over ten days.

I prep my nose for the impending stench (by now, both Johnny and Hugh smell like opium ass), crawl into the drug hut, and grab a sliver of mat in between the two of them, shifting promptly into my gentle "talking to an addict" tone.

"Hey, guys. What do you say we pack up and move on?"

Johnny looks up at me with watery eyes. Still beautiful, even in their vacancy.

"We like it here, Iris."

"I know you do, sweetheart, but we've been here over a week and there's so much stuff to see! Remember, we spoke about going down to the islands?"

"We like it here, Iris."

Well, this is going swell. I take Johnny's hand and give him the best puppy-dog look I can muster. He smiles at me, somewhat more alert.

"Pleeeeeease, Johnny?"

"Just go if you want to, Iris, we're not stopping you."

Thud. The weight of his dismissal descends upon me. It stings. It burns. It crystallizes all the horrible truths I've managed to ignore: Johnny and Hugh could stay here for months. My poor mother is worried sick. And I can't take this monotonous South Bronx–like existence a minute longer. Worst of all: Johnny hasn't given a shit about me since the day I met him. Did I know that already? Perhaps I did. Love is rarely a two-way street. Oh God. What was my wretched ass thinking, chasing after these good-for-nothing vegetables?

My long overdue outburst emerges, unrehearsed.

"*What* did you just say, Johnny?"

"I said just go if you like."

"*Go?* You're saying I can just *go?* We're on the top of a *fucking mountain*, Johnny! In the middle of bloody nowhere, *John-ee!* I don't know the fucking way! And even if I *did* know the fucking way, there's a real chance I'd get shot down by a sniper for accidentally stepping on his poppy plant! Now, how the *fuck* am I supposed to just *go*?!"

Success. The boys are jolted out of their comas, their pupils snapping back to normal diameter. They sit up, dumbstruck, waiting for my next, possibly violent, move.

Johnny takes a beat to adjust to his unfamiliar state of alertness. My heart is beating a mile an anxious minute. He takes a rejuvenating inhale and delivers the blow.

"It's your choice, Iris," he says, in a smooth, patronizing drone. "You're a free woman."

"Yeah . . . free to be killed and mutilated!" Hugh jokes, pleased at his masterful wit.

I storm out before the urge to stick the pipe up his ass becomes a reality. The tribe members watch me curiously as I stampede across the porch toward nowhere in particular. Johnny's right, I guess. I *am* a free woman. But what am I supposed to do with that information? I'm stranded here, I have no options. What's freedom without options?

I find Chief sitting on his front stoop chewing on a betel nut. I speak slowly, attempting a request in broken Akha, dismantling enough riddles to construct a sentence.

"Help me chicken get out of rooftop please."

His stare covers a wide emotional spectrum, from impatience to indifference to "What'd you just say you idiot?" I point to the jungle and make a little walking man on my palm. Chief nods, spitting a betel-nut lugey near my foot. I ask again, trying to find the word for "guide," but keep choking up every time it dawns on me that I might actually be stuck here indefinitely. A teardrop begins to emerge from it's duct, but with a forceful squeeze of my temples

I manage to suck it back into my head. My body starts shaking in releasatory anxious compensation, frustrated I won't let the pain escape through the usual channels.

My little walking man falls to his knees, crying, "Get me out of here, please, I beg you!" before collapsing in my palm. The chief looks at my dead fingers, and at long last offers a comprehending gleam. He grabs my shoulder and barks out a command into the air. Silence. He barks again, whereupon his son, Chief Junior, a rebellious acne testostewonder in acid-wash denim emerges from his hut, adjusting the American flag bandana on his head in an agitated fashion. Junior struts over, as if being pulled by a cockstring. Personally, I never liked Junior. I've always felt that he never fully appreciated my riddling skills, never offering even a courtesy laugh. Now all of a sudden he's checking me out, unabashedly staring at my perky bosom and sculpted thighs.

A dialogue ensues between father and son. I don't understand what they're saying, except that it's about me, the jungle, and my right breast. Junior's eyes light up. Help me out here, guys. What's going on? Are we talking a sex-for-exit type of exchange? Am I to be pimped out? Inducted into the tribe? What's next? Clitoridectomy? Banana pancake class?

Junior bolts back to his hut. Chief nudges me to follow. At this point I'm ready to fuck a Thai teen just to get out of here. Who knows, maybe my de-virgination will be told in riddle form for generations of budding Akhas to come.

Chapter Fourteen

Junior's hut is darker than the others. I can barely make out a bamboo mat . . . a blanket . . . a smoking pipe . . . a Vespa. What the hell is a Vespa doing in this land of head-dress and outhouse? Does the Akha budget council really believe running drugs is more important than running water? I guess so.

Junior mounts the Vespa like a ninja, replete with battle cries and martial sound effects. Per his instructional head snap, I hop on the back, still unclear on what we're doing. He bursts through the hut door with perilous bravado, forcing me to grab his waist for balance. Sly bastard.

The loud putt-putting lures the villagers out to witness my departure. They stand there as a tribal unit—one body, many faces. It hits me just then that I am really leaving. I look at them sadly, preemptively nostalgic. Johnny and Hugh are not among the crowd. Of course. But I don't care. Really, I don't. My days of wasted emotion are over. I'm on my way out and up.

Down the steep trail out of the village we go. Junior pauses at the jungle entrance for a bandana adjustment. I turn around and look back up at the drug hut for the last time. And then I see him, standing there on the porch: my love, wrapped in a sarong, a soft smile on his face. He lifts his arm slowly. "Good-bye!" he mouths, his wave growing with speed and emotion, tears in his eyes. I'd like to think they're tears of sadness, but they're probably just his corneas reacting to their first dose of sunlight in a week. Either way they're good enough for me.

I blow him a kiss, my well of emotion still ample. Oh, how I love this messedupdrugaddictedwhorefuckingbadtoothedgem of a human being. And maybe he loves me, too. I guess I'll never know.

I've never ridden into the physical and mental unknown with such velocity. Is there no such thing as a jungle speed limit? Junior is creeping me out. I feel dirty just touching the man for safety purposes. At any moment he could stop this puppy and have his way with me on the side trail. I've tried not to think about that, though, spending the last hour focusing on his volcanic face instead, ranking his zits by size and girth.

Our route seems overly circuitous, probably because Junior's making a point of passing through every single village on the way, screaming out to his friends to come outside and "check me out." Come on, Biff, does the whole goshdarn jungle have to know we're going steady?!

When we arrive in Chiang Rai, Junior pulls up by a rickety guesthouse and nudges me off the bike. The moment of truth. I brace myself and wait for him to dismount, but he just stares at me. The staring continues for about a minute. What the hell is he waiting for—money? Am I going to get fucked *and* have to pay for it? Junior's narrow hostile eyes slit even further. I take some baht and hold them out in offering, but Junior just kicks into gear and drives off, leaving me there like a rejected streetwalker.

On the curb here now I quietly stand, alone once again. But this time different. *I'm* different. No longer the child devastated when Daddy walked out the door, or when Patrick or Boaz or Johnny or the dozens of other guys kept fulfilling the prophecy that abandonment was all I could expect from men in my life. I am here alone because I have made a choice to be so. Perhaps I've been making that choice longer than I'd like to admit.

I enter my room and plop on the bed in standard T formation. My finger instinctually makes its way down to my usual source of comfort—this time focused, relaxed, and ready to rock. But I am not. Sorry, buddy, I think I'm gonna wait for the real thing. Fingie bends in understanding and rests quietly beside me. I close my eyes, knowing that tomorrow it will be pointing me in the right direction.

Right direction my ass. I have as much vivo-vector as an amoeba on crack. I'm just alone again lying in some random bed in some Godforsaken city when what I'm supposed to be doing is traveling through Asia with a bunch of friendly youth. I have nobody to blame but myself, constantly plunging myself through death and danger's door and then wondering why nobody's along for the ride.

Maybe I'm really a hermit. Maybe I crave this horrible solitude. Or maybe I need to get on a bus to Bangkok and return to backpacker civilization. If I leave right now, I can still catch the midnight express.

Chapter Fifteen

I've decided to take the VIP bus this time around. After all I've been through, I deserve it. This is the life. Padded seats. Free bag of fish rinds.* Love ballads blasting over the bus PA system all night long.

And guess what? There's not a single backpacker on the whole bus. I couldn't have inserted myself into a more alienating situation. I scan the passengers, hoping to encounter one of my local Thai whore buddies. God knows I've met enough of them. Maybe Salong or Krung Kwai is en route to the big city, chasing some empty Phat Phong dream. What a great musical that would make: *Banana Aspirations—Mastervag Returns*.

Alas, none of my Thai lovelies are in sight.

I'm all alone. It's a long, musical twelve hours, but as we roll up to the familiar bus stop at Kao San Road, relief coats my cramped muscles. I'm home. I saunter down the street, making a point of rubbing up against every single backpacker I pass, relishing the physical contact. The backpackers seem different somehow. They're actually acknowledging me—smiling, nodding, even saying hello unprompted. What the hell's different? Wait a minute. It's not them, it's me. My

---

*It seems the rich Thais eat the same weird crap as the poor ones.

adventures and ordeals have endowed me with the confident swagger of a seasoned traveler. Now that I think about it, I've been through more crazy shit in two weeks than *they* have in a year—Himalaya *that* buddy!

With this glorious insight, I check into the Sweetie Guesthouse (Down with the Melody and its wood paneling!) then cockily amble over to Thai World, where I take my usual corner table and order my banana shake–BLT combo with blasé authority (the most intimidating kind). Awestruck, the waitress rushes to fill my order and alert the lowly kitchen staff of my arrival.

Yep, things are definitely a-changin'. I haven't even gotten my first BLT and already someone has made eye contact. Not only that, this someone is a pencily Italian man with matted hair and yellow eyes. This person is a man at the top of the Asian backpacker hierarchy.

```
       THE OFFICIAL BACKPACKER HIERARCHY
                (top to bottom)


    #1. English or Italian dread-headed,
barefoot  drug  addicts;  usually  have
bones that protrude through their soiled
clothes, and teeth that are inherently
crooked and tinted from all the drugs
taken in India; possess a tranquil yet
intimidating demeanor; have been roaming
Asia for at least five years; no traceable
family members.
    #2. Gorgeous, long-legged girls with
great tans, usually Brit or Aussie; of
supermodel caliber; graduates of the Goa
```

rave scene in India and can usually be found donning colorful midriff-baring outfits to prove it; bitchy and aloof; threatening.

#3. Buff Israeli men, übermasculine former commandos with great bodies; appeal highly to the #2s for their exoticity and good personal hygiene, hence the abundant copulation between the two groups; #1s harbor no resentment regarding this fact as they are too busy worrying about their next fix.

#4. Hot Israeli girls; attitudinal firecrackers with mid- to large-sized asses and pretty faces; occasionally juggie breasted; not nearly as hot as their #2 foreign counterparts, but they're not worried; Once #3s get the #2s out of their sexual system, they dump them and end up mating with #4s, who are able to provide wilder sex without the English-speaking requirement. #3s eventually marry #4s and cheat on them many years later with #2s at some random location in Europe on a business trip.

#5. Israfros; only come to Asia for the LSD, raves, and potential #2 encounters; couldn't care less about culture and sightseeing; always travel in packs, speak very loudly with much chutzpah and self-entitlement; hated both by the snobbier #3s, desperate #4s, and polite #6s,

and are a last resort for those #2s who
have lost their #3s and still want dark-
skinned exotic enjoyment.

#6. Geeks, dorks, hikers, non-weed
smokers, and assorted annoying types; all
nationalities; used by the higher-ranking
members of the hierarchy for their knowledge of terrain and medical supplies; Israeli #6s are always equipped with a
black backpack labeled ISSTA, which is
the Israeli student travel agency. Everyone gets the bag free when they purchase
a ticket from the agency. The only difference is #3s, #4s, and #5s discard it
upon receipt, whereas #6s embrace it with
enthusiasm, wearing it out to a pulp.

What an honor to be acknowledged by the heaviest of
the heavies. I shall invite him over to my table. Just as soon
as I finish this slab of bacon. Oh wait, he's glancing at someone coming in. My competition? Not a chance. She's a newbie. A #6, big time. Israeli no doubt. Her body: plump and
awkward. Her gait: heavy. Her shiny hiking boots: still
reeking of fresh rubber and receipts. Her jam-packed money
belt: clearly busting out from beneath her layered waist. Her
pants: a pair of drawstrings boasting a pattern of mint green
tortoises (as if Walt Disney had thrown up on them, knowing Jews would be wearing them at a later date). She's so
new, I'll bet she's got her travelers cheque numbers tattooed
across her chest for safekeeping. Oh, and of course, let's not
forget the icing on the cake: the ISSTA backpack.

Good God. Doesn't she know how ridiculous she looks?! I

exchange an exaggerated eye roll with Gino Smackino. Ahh, to mock the #6s, what fun! She looks at me with oblivious confidence, a huge smile on her face. Oh no, I think I just smiled back. Go back! Turn back! I didn't mean it—it was an accident! A reflex, a cursed part of my socialization! Now she's walking toward me. Toward *my table*! Why do I never have control over who approaches my table? Dammit! I've worked very, very hard to attain my seasoned air of gloat, there is no way I'm letting you jeopardize my newfound respect within the community! For Chrissake woman, U-turn!

The only option now at my disposal is avoidance. I shoot my gaze down to my beverage, hoping Newbie will cart her happy tortoises to the ladies room. No such luck.

"Hello there!" she says, her coast-to-coast smile still pasted on her face. My banana shake is proving to be utterly fascinating right now. I grunt a barely audible hello through my straw-filled mouth.

"You been in Thailand long?" she asks.

I look around. Gino Smackino has fled the scene, and the other patrons have moved on to more interesting topics, so I venture to reply, slightly more audible this time, still staring at the bottom of my glass.

"Yes. I have."

"I just got here," she says.

"I know."

Her smile gets bigger—didn't think that was possible.

"Wow! How can you tell?"

I laugh with a "Well, *I* just got back from getting lost in the jungle secondhand-smoking opium trying to get fucked by a whore-fetishizing Englishman" look on my face.

"The ISSTA bag gives it away," I say, opting for the obvious reason, rather than insulting her perturbing sense of fashion.

"My name is Iris!" she says. "What's yours?"

Good God. Of all the names in the world, this #6 had to have mine.

"Do you know the slut's name?" Nanette asked me. Nanette was my mother's best friend. She took sadistic pleasure in presenting questions to me about my father's Puerto Rican girlfriend on a weekly basis. I quickly looked over at my mother. She just stood there with an odd smile on her face. "No, I don't," I replied, realizing that my parents had never mentioned it.* Girlfriend had obviously not gotten around to dropping off a business card.

"Do you?" I asked nervously.

"Rebecca," Nanette replied, laughing maniacally.

I stood there, stunned. Not because I was expecting her name to be Consuela or Lourdes or Juanita, and not because "Rebecca" had a funny ring to it, like Gertie or Velda, and not because Nanette was laughing so hard a breeze of warm brie was blowing over me. But because Rebecca was my mother's name. My father had found the only Puerto Rican on the planet with the same name as his wife. "At least he doesn't have to worry about getting names mixed up in bed!" Nanette drizzled on with giddy verve. "So like him to not want to waste memory cells!" She continued. I looked over to my mother once again. She was laughing along, biting into a peach. I smiled and let out a laborious chuckle,

---

*Assuming, perhaps, that the presence of the nameless is somehow less present.

happy to see my mother smile and wanting so much to make light of this creepy coincidence, but I couldn't help feeling I'd be betraying my father if I did so. I curbed my confusing urge to come to his defense, not wanting to ruin any temporary feelings of empowerment my mother was enjoying, and wishing I could enjoy some myself.

Here I am in Thai World ten years later, presented with a coincidence of equally disturbing ilk. The question is, do I disclose it? Iris will probably view the trivial commonality as a sign of instant sisterhood, and we can't have that.

"My name is Iris," I mumble nonchalantly, but for naught, for upon receipt of this information, Tortoise erupts with an "Oh my God!! *Your* name is Iris, *too?* That's so cool!!!"

I must end this conversation immediately. I reach into my back pocket and pull out fifty baht. Iris's mouth gapes at the carefree manner in which I both store and retrieve my money.

"You just keep it in your back pocket like that?" she asks.

"Money belts are for kids," I say, hurrying out. She hobbles after me.

"Wish I could chat, but I'm heading back to my guesthouse for a nap," I say.

"Oh, where are you staying?" she asks, oblivious to my tone and body language, which now consists of literally turning the other way when I mumble my responses.

"The Sweetie Guesthouse."

I have no doubt that she's also staying at the Sweetie. Probably in the adjacent room. Actually with my luck, probably under my bed.

"That's so funny!" she screams. "I'm staying at the Sweetie, too!"

It's hard being right all the time.

The smile has now extended beyond the borders of her face.

"That's great. Really. Anyway I'll see you arou—"

"I'm going to Vietnam in two days," she says, her eyes alight.

"Vietnam?" I ask, surprised and actually a little impressed. Vietnam is the least backpacked country in the region, for a plethora of reasons: travel is highly restricted by the Vietnamese government, the DMZ is still riddled with leftover mines, and even though it has been almost twenty years since the war ended, the whole country's still engulfed in a "battles in the midst" dangerous air—which, thanks to Hollywood's successful morphing of a horrible war into sexy, glistening Dafoes screaming gooks and glory amid übercool Hendrixian riffs, is exactly what makes going there so appealing.*

This newbie was gutsy. And smart, too, I discover, as she begins to spout out various facts on the history of Vietnam, not to mention its people, terrain, climate trends, and acclaimed writers (the translated works of whom she made sure to read before her departure).

"Well, have a good time," I say and keep walking,

---

*For some reason Israel has never filmically glorified or sexified its wars like America has, which is interesting considering Israel has a lot more wars to choose from. It may be precisely because Israel is fraught with nonstop bloodshed on its own soil that it can't fathom it as entertainment. Or maybe it's just a cultural mind-set, and Israelis simply don't glorify violence like Americans do, thereby having no desire to re-create exhilarating battle sequences from the Yom Kippur War to the tune of "All Along the Watchtower." Or maybe they just don't have the budget.

reflecting on how little I know about my own country's writers and climate trends. Must remedy that.

A second later I feel a tap on my shoulder.

"Wanna come?"

I stop. A moment of contemplation. Travel with Turtlepant? My gut instinct is screaming, "What are you crazy?!" But my secondary instinct, also known as my mature voice of reason, tells me, "You'd never have gone to Vietnam with Boaz! This is opportunity knocking—a sane, hygienic human who wants your companionship. Come on. She's got *responsible* written all over her; she's blessed with the fresh anal concerns of a newbie and a powerful desire to explore unchartered waters. Her face is void of malice and her air is welcoming. Her eyes, enthused as they are, exhibit a healthy mind and a curious demeanor. A trip with her could be interesting and comfortably not edgy. Like an ABC after-school special."

"I . . . I'll think about it," I say, wanting a few more minutes to assess my assessment.

"Take your time," she says, smiling her bubbly butt back into Thai World.

An hour later there's a heavy pounding on my door. I open it, startled to find Iris once again fully exploring the color spectrum. I tell her to wait while I get dressed, making sure to choose a light taupe combo to counterbalance her demented travel ensemble.

Together we proceed to the Kim Travel Agency, run by Kim the Travel Agent. Kim Travel Agency is one of the select agencies on Kao San Road lucky enough to possess the coveted storefront sign that reads:

MOOMLATZ

Moomlatz is the Hebrew word for "recommended." It is the business owner's way of telling the world that "Israelis were here, and in exchange for my not fucking them over pricewise, they made a sign for me in Hebrew that would lure more Israelis to come, which is crucial considering Israelis comprise 99 percent of the traveling population and are therefore the most important source of clientele, which is great, except for the fact that Israelis drive a really hard bargain and are so paranoid about being fucked over it's insulting—perhaps it's a Holocaust complex, or behavioral remnants from the Communist era, or just a legitimate fear of anti-Semitism that stems from a stereotype of frugality and suspicion that is more than partially accurate."

The point is, the signs work.*

On the wall, Kim has hung Polaroid photos of herself with every Israeli who has ever purchased a ticket from her office. There are hundreds of them. And they're all smiling. What a relief. In a sea of frauds, Kim's moomlatz is the real deal.

She happily issues us a round-trip ticket on Vietnam Air, in to Saigon, out from Hanoi. Just saying that makes me feel cool. Vietnam Air is apparently a very new airline with very old airplanes. Iris and I are both a little worried about this, only I'm trying not to show it.

"Is that a decent airline, Kim?" Iris asks.

"Yes, yes, very good, very good. Moomlatz! Moomlatz!"

---

*When it comes to advice on not getting fucked over, one Israeli's word to another is as good as gold. It's all part of the "us against them/everyone hates the Jews" mentality. The fact is, Israelis will only trust each other. Except when they're actually in Israel, of course, where they wouldn't trust each other with the time of day.

Kim smiles and pulls out her Instamatic, ready to eternalize our purchase.

The *M* word in oral form puts Iris immediately at ease, and she begins to gussy up for her photo-op. I turn around and reluctantly put my arm around her for the shot, praying her reptilian trousers aren't in frame.

We've been waiting on the tarmac for so long, I fear the pilot is perusing the Airbus manual. As I expected, there are only a few other backpackers on the flight, and they're all Israeli. There's Danit, a dykie young girl with a shaved head who bears a marshmallow-like resemblance to Sinead O'Connor, and two guys straight out of *Goodfellas: Haifa*. The one, a lanky, freckled redhead; the other, a sweet-faced yam of a man—so bland, a stick-figure rendering would be overly expressive.

Iris bonds with the threesome right off the seat buckle, launching into an animated debate on Fuji versus Kodak. I, on the other hand, sit quietly, opting instead to plan my disengagement upon our arrival in Saigon.

We've finally started jetting down the runway. It's about time. Seems Vietnam Air does not believe in standard take-off procedure; after only three seconds of taxi, our pilot spears us skyward at a ninety-degree angle. My stomach does a reverse cannonball into my throat and I compress my face onto the window, making some joke about this being a *Top Gun* audition. Iris laughs nervously beside me. I can feel her looking at the back of my head, waiting for a commiseratory response, but I just keep staring out into the diagonal sky, praying we don't exit the stratosphere by accident.

Vietnam

Chapter Sixteen

Fuck me hard with a triangular straw hat. The streets of Saigon are insane. They make Bangkok look like Boca. The pavement is barely visible from all the millions of cyclos, mopeds, pedestrians, dogs, and baguettes flooding the streets. Into every major intersection they propel themselves with gusto, in full oblivion of anyone around them, miraculously able to transcend the laws of physics and come out the other side unscathed, untouched, without so much as a shoulder brush. I can't even bike in an empty parking lot without knocking into someone's testicles.

The official currency of Vietnam is the dong. That's right. The money here is named after cock. And we just made our first million of it. Literally. We walked in to exchange some money, and came out with over one million cock. Brilliant. *Not* so brilliant is the fact that the Vietnamese treasury apparently believes in only printing denominations of five- and ten-dong bills, thereby forcing us to receive our riches in numerous rubber-banded cockblocks, conveniently packaged in large paper bags. Mom would be pleased.

Choosing a guesthouse is an easy task, considering there's only one government-approved tourist hotel in the whole city. It's a cement compound with the charm of a rehab clinic. The reception is bare and unwelcoming with cold tile floors and fluorescent lighting that highlights the pale blue walls. The lack of any MOOMLATZ! signage leads me to believe we might just be the first Israelis to check in here.

Our room is surprisingly large and just as sterile as Reception. A ceiling fan oscillates unsteadily, slowly stirring the stale air in microscopic waves, teetering on the brink of collapse with every rotation.

We dump our brown paper bags onto the bed like groceries. As Iris begins to unpack, I contemplate my next move, but am quickly interrupted by yet another one of her delighted outbursts.

"Danit's hired a cyclo for the whole day tomorrow, we're meeting her downstairs at eight A.M. Isn't that *fantastic?*" she cries, piling her little money blocks into organized pyramids on her pillow.

"Yes, that's great!" I reply, discreetly setting my alarm for six. What a relief. Danit has now removed the guilt-latch from my Iris Emergency Exit Door. Iris was officially taken care of, and I could do as I pleased without her. Of course, I didn't really have to plan a sneak getaway, I could've just as easily told her that I wanted to spend the day alone, but alas, I'm not as mature and well adjusted as that.

6:17 A.M. The way I just tiptoed out the door, you'd think I was slinking off to make out with the middle-aged next-door neighbor in the tool shed.

The streets are already packed with Namsters on their way to work. The sky is a sleepy grayish blue, the sun too lazy to make an appearance just yet. I love this time of day; it adds that extra sense of discovery, as if I'm the first person alive today to see anything.

I find a scowling cycloman to pedal me around the whole day for five dollars. The cheeky bastard wants six, but I haggle him down a buck. I know, I know, a buck is nothing for me but a shitload for him, but think about it, he's making more from me in one day than he usually makes in a whole month!*

I board the primitive contraption and he pedals into the fray.

One thing is for certain. Cyclos are not for Jews. Who knew a mode of transportation could involve so much *guilt?* How are you supposed to enjoy the ride when the driver's sweating like a dog from pedaling your fat ass, cringing at every turn?

I'm tempted to offer my assistance and take his place on the bike for a while, but I eventually overcome this urge and resign to limiting my manifestations of guilt to wincing every time he stops to readjust his spine—which turns out to be every two minutes or so.

The first stop on our day tour is the War Museum, or as the Vietnamese call it, the *See How the Bastard Americans Fucked Us Up Museum.* Nammy leaves me by the entrance doors, which have only just opened. I'm the first one here. Very cool.

Inside, the whole place smells like sixth-grade science lab. There's not much on display except for a few photos of war-torn villages taped to the wall and a large glass jar in the corner. Something is suspended inside, floating in what I assume is formaldehyde. I move in closer.

---

*Standard tourist justification for being cheap with locals. Another one is "My money goes a much longer way here, so it's really worth as much to me as it is to them."

Good God.

It's a baby. With two heads. Staring back at me through the liquid preservative. It looks like a sci-fi movie prop, but my stomach assures me otherwise.

The baby and I stare at each other. An oddly intimate and sad exchange. My heart aches at the sight of its bulging eyes, begging me to release its body from this eternal hell, frozen forever in this freakish state. Just as bad is the hand-written label underneath: AGENT ORANGE. The poor creature's whole existence has been reduced to a result, a mere toxic ingredient.

Has the baby not suffered enough? Must it also be used as a device aimed merely to elicit a visceral response to the horrible acts committed by Americans during the war? This gut-wrenching display only compounds the very suffering and disgrace it aims to condemn!

I painfully head toward the exit. Mission accomplished, my friendly curators. I'm going to be sick.

Exiting this little shop of horrors, the sunlight hits me with an undue harshness, only accentuating my budding melancholy. Nammy's waiting for me by the limo. I hold back my urge to apologize to him for the war, however absurd such an apology would be. I'm just happy he doesn't think I'm American.

Otherwise, I never would've been able to haggle him down.

It's already lunchtime, and I ask Nammy to take us to an establishment of his choice. It turns out to be a street-side shithole a block away. A chaotic tarp hovers over four long picnic benches, each packed with Vietnamese workers chowing down on some amorphous sludge from large tin bowls.

As we approach, the penised mass gives me an incredulous stare. You'd think I'd be somewhat intimidated by fifty men ogling me like that. But thanks to that wonderful thing both they and I possess, I'm completely at ease. It's called sexual repression.

My date orders for the two of us, and we promptly receive bowls filled with what everyone else is having: chicken and rice.

Just so you know, that whole term "tastes like chicken" is bullshit. In reality, chicken tastes like nothing. It has *no* flavor. None. Nada. Nicht. I ask the guys at the table for some salt or soy sauce, but they stare at me blankly and proceed with their banter. Unlike my previous Akhan foray into foreign language communication, this time I can't even remotely gauge what these guys are talking about; their cadence is so monotonous that distinguishing between jokes and laments is impossible. For all I know they're discussing the prospect of sticking a chopstick up my ass.

At last, we bid adieu to the teamsters and slog back to the cyclo. Nammy's in a food coma and can barely walk. I, however, could eat a fucking horse. The chicken fiesta was equivalent to a three-course meal of air as far as my stomach's concerned. Thankfully, we pass this little stand on the corner that sells baguettes smothered in that triangular La Vache Qui Rit cheese. God bless the French occupation.

From Nammy's incessant mumbling, I gather his hernia's acting up. Fine, I tell him, let's call it a day, I'm tired anyway. The ride back is excruciatingly slow and vocal. New groaning sounds have entered into the mix. By the time the hotel is in sight, Nammy has jumped off his bike seat and is pushing the cyclo from behind. I couldn't feel more ridiculous. I can just imagine the faces he's making as I sit there with my dorky pouch on my lap, trying to maintain a semblance of humility.

With a final grunt we come to a halt. Before I can dismount with dignity, he tips the cyclo over and I come tumbling out, barely landing on my feet. Poor man. Labor-driven sweat has eroded his face, as if it were acid emitting from his pores. All because of me. If I were him, I would've kicked my ass out on the street a long time ago.

I tip him a few extra cock, gladly taking conscience-credit for feeding his family for the next three months, and head back into the hotel.

When I get to the room, I find a note from Turtle on the door:

> *Where'd you go?*
> *I'm off with Danit and the boys. See you later.*

Thwack! The face of jealous regret has reared its ugly head. Yes, *I* was the one who didn't want to join them, but now that they've gone without me, I wish I had. God, I'm a freak. Forget the whole "grass is greener" syndrome—I seem to deny the other side even has grass until I've mowed my own lawn into a pulp. But enough whining and weird metaphors, woman. You wanted to meet new people, get your ass back on the streets and do it. You'll deal with your inability to ever be happy or at peace with your decisions later. Social Saigon awaits.

Chapter Seventeen

Unlike Bangkok, Saigon has only two Thai World–style backpacker hangouts: the Kim Café right outside the hotel, and the Sinh Café directly across it. From what I've heard, once you sit at one café, you're committed to it and it's considered bad form to cross over to the other. A political affiliation of sorts.

Armed with my requisite "nomad introspection journal" (surprising what small objects can do for one's confidence), I take a corner table at Kim Café (it was closer) and assess the situation. It doesn't take long. The only other person in the joint is a surfer dude sitting in the corner, looking very out of a place. He's writing furiously, his socked sandals swaying under the table, his stick-straight blond hair bobbing back and forth like anorexic car-wash brushes. American, no doubt.

The waitress approaches. I make sure to crack a nifty joke about my appetite, intentionally loud enough to be heard by my fellow patron. He looks up and gleams a smile. I smile back.

"You're funny!" he says, a bounce in his voice.

"I try."

"You American?" he asks.

"No. Israeli." (As part of my all-encompassing identity crisis, I tend to fluctuate with what I define as my country of origin, always picking the country that sounds more exotic in that specific situation. Since Blondie here is obviously American, I figure Israeli is the way to go.)

"Oh," he replies. "Then how come you sound American?"

Inquisitive little bugger. So what if I'm an American citizen? So what if I spent most of my life there? That doesn't mean I'm American, does it? Yeah, well I guess it does. Time to explain myself. I just have to make sure I'm crafty in my autobiographical phraseology. Here goes.

"Well, I lived in the Bronx until I was twelve, and then moved *back* to Israel . . ." (Okay fine, I know I didn't really move *back* to Israel since I'd never lived there in the first place, but the way I see it, Israel is the motherland, and any Jew who moves there is going *back* in a sense, so in essence I'm not really lying, so lay off.)

So far he's buying it. For all he knows, I'm a full-blooded Israeli who just spent a little time break-dancing on cardboard boxes under the 6 train before returning to Israel. Time to load the bullet.

"Then, of course, I served in the *army* for two years."

"Really? Wow! The army—that's pretty fucking impressive!"

Heh heh. This time I'm not gonna fuck up the army card like I did with the Brit Brigade, I have it rehearsed, perfected, and ready for delivery.

"Yeah, I was a sergeant . . . Intelligence."

"Oh wow! What'd you do in Intelligence?"

Furrow that brow, O' Smooth One. Prep dramatic avoidance line.

"I'm sorry. I can't really talk about it."

"Oh," he says, taking a bite of his pancake. "I just met an Israeli girl in Cambodia who drove tanks."

Where the hell did that come from? Shit. On the sexy spectrum, tank driving definitely outranks intelligence. My voice wavers as I struggle to get militant bitch out of the picture.

"Oh. Tanks. Right. Well . . . I had an Uzi!"

"She had an M-16 and an AK-47, too."

Alright, time to jump to another topic.

"I'm Iris by the way."

"Seth."

We shake. His hands are not clammy. Good.

"Where are you from, Seth?"

"California."

Of course. His toothy smile bathes my banana pancakes in an ivory light. Nice to see I've moved from scuzzy Euro-kinds up to nice surfer boys with perfect teeth and no apparent drug habits.

"Did you just get here?" Seth asks.

"Yesterday."

"What are your plans?"

"Well, the only legal way to get around is to hire a van and driver and go up to Hue," I say, proud of my Lonely Planet up-read.

"You need ten people for that," he counters, obviously having read up on the matter as well.

"Ten people?"

"Yep. Let's give it a shot, dude!" He says with much merriment.

"You mean get a group together?"

"Yep."

"Sure!" I say, getting caught up in his hygienic enthusiasm. Remarkable, the skill we backpackers possess in the immediate-intimacy department. We've no hesitation about jumping in a van with ten complete strangers and spending the next month together twenty-four hours a day—a risk rarely taken in the real world, if ever.

The question now is, where do we find eight more people? And a van for that matter! Seth and I take a moment to contemplate this quandary in silence. We are interrupted by some very loud and clumsy pot-clanging sounds from the kitchen, whereupon a tall, middle-aged Vietnamese man in a brown trucker hat appears before us. His voice is Costneresque: sensually soothing, yet clipped.

"I can be driver," he says, dusting off his pants. "I am Pat" (an obvious logical derivative).

"That's great, dude!" our West Coast representative gushes.

"Dude" is not the most titillating of words; it somehow has that knack of making even a biochemist sound like an idiot. I can only imagine what the brilliant minds roaming around Caltech sound like, dude-ing each other all day long, pipettes and petri dishes in hand.

"Do we still need ten people, Pat?" I ask, eager to get in on the conversation.

"Yes, I think it best for you."

Gosh, he's so considerate.

"For money, it make it more cheap for you. You Israeli, no? You like cheap!"

Ahh. I guess my people *have* managed to carve out some kind of local reputation after all. Good going, children of Zion.

"Where are we going to find eight more people?" I ask him.

Right on cue, as if sent from above, a trio of perfectly tanned German girls enter the Kim Café.*

I've never been the biggest fan of Germans, not only for the obvious "Hey, we have a not-so-great-history, your people and I" kind of way, but also because I've never clicked with their (lack of) humor. Dry wit seems to not be part of the überland's mentality. But maybe these girls were different.

"Um, excuse me," I say sweetly. They look at one another, as if I were some skanky guy in a dive bar asking to slow dance, and they were all trying to avoid the offer without being rude, hoping one girl would chime in an acquiescent response and save the rest. I wait a beat before treading on with my query.

"Are you girls heading up to Hue by any chance?"

The six-foot, more petite member of the bunch replies.

"Yes, we are going to Hue. Why do you ask?"

"Well, I have a driver, and I'm trying to muster up ten people to split the cost, so if you're interested, we plan on leaving tomorrow."

"Super! We'll talk it over for a moment."

"Oh, okay."

I stand there like an idiot waiting for her college acceptance letter. I turn to Seth, but he's not in his seat. Was he not part of the effort all of a sudden? I spot him across the street tossing around a hackeysack with Pat. There is nothing more

---

*How the hell do these Aryan types tan so well? My Mediterranean skin always turns seven different shades of brown before breaking out, peeling, or splotching two days later. Meanwhile, these goddesses of fair skin and snowmobiles roam Asia with perfectly bronzed bodies. It's just not right.

disturbing than seeing a somewhat plump Vietnamese man trying to maneuver a hackeysack.

A tap on my shoulder breaks my horrified stare.

"We're in!" the girls cry in friendly unison.

Yay! They are nice after all! Their grandparents were the ones who helped the Jews, I just know it.

"I'm Aksel!" the tall brunette says, giving me her hand to shake.

"Hi, Aksel, I'm Iris."

"This is Else and Kari. We're from Norway."

Guess I was wrong about the über alles thing. Tan threw me off.

"Nice to meet you," I say in earnest. "Are you staying here as well?"

Considering it's the only guesthouse in Saigon, the question sounds stupid, but dammit, I have a driver and I won't be made to feel silly.

"Yes. We are in room 605." Aksel replies. "Oh, how much is the van?"

Good question. I guess I jumped the gun, wrangling up the troops before acquiring adequate information.

"We, um, haven't decided that yet."

I rush over to the hackeysack tournament. Pat has now succumbed to imitating Seth's expression and is maneuvering his feet with full white-man's overbite.

I aggressively tap Pat on the back with *I could have driven a tank if I wanted to!* gusto.

"How much is this van going to cost us, Pat?" (And what the hell is your real name anyway? It's not like some putz at Ellis Island made you change it from Mao-Vin into Frank—I mean you live in Vietnam for Chrissake, you have no excuse for a name like Pat.)

Pat makes a very strained facial expression, indicating to us that a huge sacrifice on his part is imminent.

"For you . . . let's see . . . fifty thousand dong."

Oh come on, don't talk to me in dong, my man. I close my eyes to compute. This is going to take forever. I suck at math and now everyone's gonna know it. I could use some help here, Quicksilver.

"*Fifty thousand,* dude?" Seth says, tossing the hackeysack to Pat for punctuation. "That seems a little rough. Hook us up, man. How about twenty thousand dong?"

Pat is somewhat surprised at Seth's audacity. Especially after their shared overbite experience.

"Forty thousand," Pat retorts.

"Twenty-five thousand, bro?"

"Thirty thousand."

"Twenty-five thousand, boss?"

"Yes. Twenty-five thousand. But I don't guide in each city, only drive, and you buy me food."

Okay.

"Sounds good, my man," Seth says as they shake hands. It is in fact a good deal.

"Yes, that's fine with me!" I bark, making sure to assert some authority now, before my lack of tankhood makes Seth step all over me.

I go back to Oslo with the exciting price news. They are a go. Aksel mentions a nice Englishman named Freddie who's in the room next door to theirs as a possible van mate as well. We all agree to reconvene in an hour and I head back to the hotel. As I'm crossing the street, I spot Iris and her posse dramatically turn the corner, walking in a slo-mo line, kind of like *The Outsiders* gone awry. In Matt Dillon's position is Iris, clad in frog-infested trousers (I wonder if she has a pair

for each of the ten plagues), flanked by Danit and the Goodfellas, who are gaiting as if chasing a man who stabbed them
only moments earlier: determined, yet wobbly.

I had completely forgotten about them. Four bodies that
had totally slipped my mind, two of which I was actually
sharing a room with. Now I know I planned on ditching
Iris the minute I got here, but four bodies is four bodies,
and it's not like she's been so bad up until now. At least we
could rely on her posse to not display any hackeysack skills
or yelps of "Dude!"

Iris's face lights up as she sees me. "Hey Iris!" she yells,
waving frantically to me from afar.

The fourth grade. I was a child growing up in the Bronx.
Out of my Israeli parents' desire to provide me with a Jewish education, they enrolled me at an Orthodox Jewish
school. Interesting choice, considering my parents were
ridiculously secular. Since everybody in the school was
highly Orthodox except me, the only way I was to be ac-
cepted by my classmates was to pretend my family was Orthodox, too. And so began the lie I was forced to sustain
from the minute I stepped into my first-grade class.

Keeping up this fallacy was a draining task, especially
for a child. I had to find reasons for everything, from my
absence from the neighborhood shul every Shabbes ("My
parents make me go to a *super*-Orthodox shul that nobody
knows about . . .") to why my family only had one sink for
both meat and milk dishes ("We don't eat milk").

And so years went by with me anxiously keeping up the
illusion, constantly terrified I'd be found out and banished
accordingly. Obviously the pressure of living a lie at such

a young age was enormous, and every time my parents took me to the neighborhood McDonald's, I ducked down in the backseat, lest a schoolmate spot me entering the parking lot.

The hardest thing for me was missing The Riverdale Jewish Center's weekly Shabbes event, because my family was too busy dragging me to Manhattan to eat pork and go to the Guggenheim.

But thankfully, one morning, after much pleading, my mother allowed me to participate. I made a big deal of it at school, telling everyone how I didn't have to go to the special shul that week, and how I could finally come hang out at the RJC. I couldn't wait.

That Saturday morning I woke up at the crack of dawn, put on my best down-to-the-floor skirt, and prepared to walk to the RJC about a mile away.

"Are you ready?" my mother asked, grabbing the car keys.

"What are you doing, Ima? I'm walking."

"No, you're not walking, I'm driving you."

"*Ima!* You know we're not supposed to be driving on Shabbes!"

"Oh, stop with that nonsense."

My anxiety levels were rising by the millisecond.

"Ima, you *promised* you'd let me do this, please don't ruin it for me!"

"Fine, fine, but I'm picking you up at four P.M."

"Ima, you're not listening to me. I CAN'T BE SEEN GETTING INTO A CAR. EVERYONE THINKS WE'RE ORTHODOX!"

"You shouldn't care what they think," she says.

"Ima, please."

"Fine, fine. I'll pick you up at four fifteen, is that better?"

"Four thirty. Everybody will be in the shul for *mincha* by then."

"Fine. Four thirty."

"And pick me up a block away. No, two blocks away."

"Fine. Two blocks away, four thirty. You happy now?"

"Thanks, Ima!" I said, relieved, giving her a big kiss and embarking on my first real Shabbes hike.

The day was fantastic. My presence at the RJC dispelled any lingering doubts that I wasn't religious. I was spending quality Jew time with my classmates and felt like my life lie was becoming truth at long last.

Everyone had just gotten done hearing Rabbi Cohn give a little Torah talk, and we were in the front courtyard chatting. I kept glancing at my watch, preparing to say my good-byes at four fifteen and walk the two blocks to my pick-up location.

I was chatting with David Silber (only the *cutest* guy in class!) when a car started to honk. Very, very loudly. We all turned to look at the obnoxious disturbance. It was a beat-up blue Ford Torino. And inside the blue Ford Torino was my mother. And just in case there was any question over her identity, she burst out in a loud call of the wild.

"EEERRRRRRREESSSSSSSSSSSSSSSE!" she howled. Repeatedly. Her arm was flailing in rhythm like a Judaica robot on speed. "EEEREESE!" wave wave, "EEEREESE!" wave wave.

Within seconds, David had run off screaming, while the rest of the class had moved two feet away from my satanic body, lest my sins rub off on them. I wanted to die. I knew that if I didn't proceed to the car immediately my mother would keep hollering my name. So I thrust my head between my legs as far as it would go and sloppily ran to the car, holding back the deluge of tears and hatred that was welling up inside me.

Perhaps that's why I'm feeling so nauseated right now at the sight of Iris's ecstatic airborne arm. I remind myself that none of these people are religious, Jewish, or hip. Here in Saigon, it is we that are considered the hipster crowd. We are the *only* crowd, for that matter. But still I'm unable to bring myself to reciprocate a wave. In lieu of such a gesture, I motion for her to approach.

"You disappeared this morning," she says.

"Sorry, I woke up early. Took a short day tour."

"How was it?" she asks, apparently not that upset by my absence.

"Great."

"How much did you pay?"

"Seven dollars with tip."

"*What?* Seven dollars! You got fucked over! We haggled the guy down to four!"

Seth laughs. "Sucker!" he says to me, shooting a Colgate to the gang.

Whose side were they on—humanity or frugality?

"Well, who cares!" I say impatiently. "I got us a van and a guide for the month, so if you guys wanna join, we're all set!"

They're in.

I debrief the A-team on the details. Everyone is very excited at the alacrity of my organizational skills.

"Okay, we leave next morning," Pat says, relieved he just funded the next six months of his existence.

"I'm going to go pack, catch you later," Seth says, planting a surprising kiss on my cheek. Tender. Clean. California.

We head back to our respective rooms. Halfway up the hotel stairs, my bowels notify me of an outgoing movement. I'd almost forgotten about them, my bowels. Could it be? Have I gone solid?

I skip my way to the bathroom. This must be my lucky day. I sit down, and for the first time since I arrived in Asia, have a nice, sturdy shit. I wipe with purpose, savoring the touch, and toss the sandpaper to its death, looking down for confirmation.

And then I see them.

Long, stringy worms hanging out the sides of my poop. I watch them as they crawl animatedly this way and that, as if the crevices of my shit were cozy alleyways in Paris.

Chapter Eighteen

"You are the first one downstairs." Pat tells me, his trucker hat looking especially refreshed this morning. We spend the time getting better acquainted. Pat asks me if my father left behind any family here before going to America. I realize he thinks my father was some GI and I'm part Vietnamese. Perhaps he's not aware that there are other nationalities that possess olive complexions and dark straight hair.

I'm tempted to play along, to tell him about my Vietnamese mother who lives in Jersey, how I never knew Daddy, but Mommy told me he was handsome and a good fighter. Instead, I ask him about his history, which, actually having happened, seems far more interesting than me sitting there fabricating factoids for my own entertainment.

Turns out Pat flew a chopper for the Americans during the war, and to this day feels uncomfortable going up north to Hanoi. For that reason, he admits to me quietly, he will only escort us up to Hue. From there we'll have to get up to Hanoi by our own devices, which he assures me should not be a problem.

Toward the van struts a very tall man, guitar strapped over his peasant-bloused shoulder. Dangling from his arm is a small colorful bag that was probably made by some Peruvian woman and purchased on his last *I'm an eternal gypsy* year-long excursion to South America.

"Are you Errrrriss?" he says, slaughtering my name, somehow managing to put equal emphasis on every syllable and creating some new ones in the process.

"You must be Freddie."

"Yes, I am." He gives me a warm handshake. His enormous smile is contagious. I just hope his huge teeth are not. At least they're white. Super white actually. I'm excited to have more than Seth as my option for this journey. It's the Brit thing, I guess. I thought I was over it, but clearly I'm not. But who can blame me? I've waited this long, of course I'd rather my penetration party involve an exotic James Bondian fantasy man than a Hang Ten poster child. So what if this particular Bond happens to wear embroidered clothing and a yin yang pendant?

Danit comes down next, followed by Iris, who's sporting a festive lilypad print.

"Hi, everybody!" Iris says with a yawn.

"Hello, Iris number one!" Freddie says, giving her a warm hug. For some reason he pronounces *her* name flawlessly.

"You know each other?" I ask, confused.

"We met last night," Freddie replies.

"Last night?" I sour. "When?"

"After you went to sleep we all went to Maxim's for a drink and played pool at Apocalypse Now."

Apocalypse Now?! Only the coolest bar listed in the Lonely Planet!

"Why didn't you wake me, Iris?" I ask with much irritation and head-bobbing.

"After that awful worm thing you told me you had, I thought you should rest," Iris replies with genuine consideration.

Great. The worm thing. We haven't started our journey and already Freddie knows I have little wormies playing hackeysack up my anus.

"What do they look like, these worms of yours?" Freddie asks with intrigue.

"Excuse me?"

"What do the worms look like?"

"Nice build, good complexion."

Freddie releases a robust laugh before getting technical on me again.

"No, really, were they long and stringy or short and fat?"

"Um, I think they were long and stringy."

"Oh, then you're fine. We should just get you some dewormers, I might have a few in my bag."

He digs into his Peruvian fiesta and pulls out a mysterious unlabeled bottle. He places three large pills in my hand that look like rabbit-shit nuggets.

"Drink up," he says, handing me a bottle of water.

I chug down the pills like the pleasing peasant that I am. As I swallow, I attempt to make sexy eyes at Freddie as we share this wonderful moment of healing. But one pill gets lodged in my trachea, and I start coughing. Nasty ugly coughs, the phlegmy, disgusting ones babies emit when you're on airplanes with them.

Freddie whacks me on the back. The pill flies out. He picks it up and hands it back to me. I brush it off and swallow again, making no attempt to look even remotely sexy at this point.

Seth shows up next. His blond hair is glistening in the sunlight; he's wearing his perfunctory socks and Tevas.

"Hey, dudes!"

"Hi, Seth!" Freddie, Danit, and Iris declare in unison.

"How you holding up after last night?" Iris asks. They share a laugh.

"Yeah, mate, how are you this morning?" Freddie chimes in.

Insert disgruntled moan here.

"Anyone see the Norwegian girls?" I burst in.

"What Norwegian girls?" Freddie asks.

Oh, thank God. They weren't there last night. There's hope for inclusion yet.

"Oh . . . the girls from Oslo. Reeeeally cute," Seth says.

"Oh, lovely, I can't wait!" Freddie says, appetite aroused.

I must reiterate that I am not threatened by other women who make me feel inadequate—I know that the person who will really love me will love me despite all of my issues. The fact that I've never loved anybody despite all of *their* issues is a different story. But that doesn't mean it couldn't happen. The fact that I can't even fathom such a human being doesn't mean it couldn't happen either.

The ladies of Oslo descend from their palace, golden brown. What were they doing last night? Sleeping in a tanning bed while I was spewing fish bait out of my ass?

"Good morning, everyone!" they say, exchanging handshakes and hugs and kisses with their newfound van mates.

I stand there like a neglected camp counselor. It dawns on me, however, that I have to spend three weeks in a van with these people and better start liking it, so I swiftly place my cute bitterness in a little tiny drawer in my heart (one with easy access) and prepare to take charge of my troops.

"Everyone, this is Pat, he will be our guide and driver. Pat, this is the group."

Pat salutes the group.

"We should get going if we want to be at Mekong Delta by dark," he says, with pointed drama. An exhilarating rush of blood pulses through our collective vein, whereupon everyone races past me into the van. Before I can pull out my *Let It Bleed* cassette, all the seats have been claimed, save for the front one next to Pat, who invites me to join him with a long-lost daughter gaze.

I pout before reluctantly taking my place in the front passenger seat. I pull down the vehicle sun-visor, or whatever the hell you call that thing, and spend the next hour just eyeing everyone through the mirror, schoolteacher-like, hoping to catch them shooting spitballs or making out in the backseat. But they're just chatting quietly amongst themselves, like the fucking adults that they are.

We get to the Mekong Delta by late afternoon. Pat takes us on a walking tour of the Cu Chi tunnels, demonstrating with glee how various booby traps and devices snapped American bodies in half. (Didn't he fight on our side?) Pat asks if anyone wants to try stepping onto a pile of leaves and plummeting into the shark-toothed trap below, to "feel what it's like, but in a safe, fun way." I look over to Seth to see if he's even remotely interested or offended. Neither. He's making karate chop moves to himself by a nearby tree.

After three exciting hours of group oohing and aahing, Pat reveals to us that the tunnels and booby traps we've just seen are re-creations of the original ones, built for tourist purposes. This confession causes great disappointment and annoyance among the group, who'd prefer not to know they schlepped across the globe to see some replicas. Pat is confused by the negative energy now emanating his way and I make an effort to explain to him the value of authenticity, commending his honesty but pointing out that it's bad for business.

The ride to Danang is tainted with cynicism and grumpiness. In an attempt to lift spirits, the Oslo Girls have embarked on a Björk singathon. But their cracked voices and fuzzy legs are not enough to pep up the group.

We near the port of Danang just as the sun is setting. It is a pretty boring colorless sunset. One minute it's really bright and light, and the next minute it's dark and starts smelling funny in the van.

My first thought is that Pat let out a nice Vietnamese fart, but that notion is dispelled when Seth declares "Dude! That was my worst yet! Awesome!" Nobody else seems to care. Perhaps they're all still wondering if this whole trip is gonna be one big rip-off.

I can't help but inhale the literal smell of dismay now permeating the van and am the first one to leap out as we roll up to our hotel, which, compared to the one in Saigon, seems to have more of a mental home rather than rehab feel to it.

The large red-lettered sign above the entryway lists two room options: *WITH* hot water for ten dollars, and *NO* hot water for eight. Iris and I take a room with hot water, and expect everyone to do the same. Much to our surprise, they do not.

Of course, within minutes of checking into our room, the whole group has lined up outside our door to use the shower. Cheap bastards. Not that I'd want them to pay me per minute of usage, but nobody likes to feel mooched for their hot water, either.

Our horrible dinner consists of shreds of bony chicken bits with some bony rice and super-sweet bony coke. After a sturdy bowel movement that takes a joyous fifteen minutes (a personal record), I head toward the hotel courtyard, where I find Freddie playing guitar and singing folk songs, his stringy, greasy brown hair swaying passionately with every strum. His voice is deep, adequately raspy, and pleasant. The man definitely has the campfire canon down, moving smoothly through Van Morrison, the Beatles, and Led Zeppelin. He has also managed to get everyone to sing along, their various accents melding into an amorphous foreigner harmonium of sorts, the NATO smores practically forming themselves.

Everyone smiles as I descend the stairs into view. I swiftly bust out with a little two-part harmony on "Scarborough Fair," much to Seth's and Freddie's admiration. Freddie segues into a solo rendition of "Brown Eyed Girl" that I can only imagine is for my benefit. We all applaud, waiting for the next number, but Freddie puts the guitar down, either because his repertory has been tapped or because he's just exhausted from all the smiling and swaying.

It's quiet now. But a bond has formed, a bond that was forged at the crappy Cu Chi tunnels and bony chicken meal and has now culminated with this awesome Garfunkelian transcension of borders. We are now ready to reveal more about ourselves.

Freddie begins. He discloses that his real name is not Freddie. It's Brian. He's only called Freddie due to his uncanny resemblance to Freddie Mercury. While I know

Freddie Mercury was a talented musician, RIP, there's no doubt that he was one of the ugliest humans I'd ever seen. I wish Brian had not chosen to share that little factoid, because now I'm unable to harken back to the glorious days when I found him attractive. All I can see now is Mr. Mercury in spandex on his deathbed. Thank God I'm sitting next to Seth at the moment.

It seems I'm not alone in my disgust—Iris and Danit declare that they're tired and off to bed. The Goodfellas, too, decide to return to their room and invite everyone to come over to smoke a joint. Within seconds Freddie has packed his guitar and is up the stairs, but not without stealing a glance at Seth and me first. In turn, Seth and I look at each other in a sort of spontaneous moment of mutual consultation, like only couples do.

"We'll stay out here for a little longer," Seth says for the two of us.

I look at Seth and smile, trying not to turn into an ogling idiot. I manage to find a happy medium, and Seth and I spend the next quiet hour in the courtyard shooting the breeze. We even dude-dude for a short while. I keep waiting for him to lean over and kiss me, but apparently that's not part of his game plan. Patience, stupid, patience. If this is the guy you're going to get intimate with, then you'd better take your time. So I wait four more minutes and then lean in for the kill, closing my eyes in an effort to lock lips with dude.

"Hey, Iris. Whoa," he says pulling a mile away in one motion of his neck.

Whoa! That's a reaction?

"I'm sorry. I'm just very attracted to you," I say, in what I hope is charming honesty.

"I think you're great, too," he replies. I don't wait to see if he means it and lean in for another kiss. But like a gay rock star who seeks an early demise, Freddie suddenly appears at the top of the stairs.

"You guys should come on up."

Seth leaps up like a gazelle and grabs my hand. I am not dismayed. On the contrary, hash is the perfect precursor to lovemaking, I tell myself, feeling a lot more comfortable around illegal herbs than I did on that first fateful night in the jungle.

The Goodfellas' room smells like smoke and feet. The dynamic duo are already baked out of their minds, snoring like only Jews can. I look over to Seth and Freddie. Such different species, these two: the hippie Englishman, the surfer Santa Barbarian. Seth takes an impressively long hit. His head tilts back to the pale blue wall, and within seconds I witness the phlegmatic demon take over his body. He's too loose now, too mushy, he can't function like this, can he? I mean Johnny was a boner festival after hash, but this is surfer dude—I've no idea what his sex drive is like, his hair is too clean. His eyes close, transporting him to some faraway bliss. I wonder if he's dreaming about the OP Pro.

Freddie laughs. "It's just you and me now, "he says invitingly from his position on the bed across the room.

I smile back at him, somehow feeling like I'm cheating on Seth by doing so. It's ridiculous. I've known Seth a total of three days. I literally just embarked on the road of flirt with him and have not even reached a pit stop, let alone a dead end. Not only that, but Seth's the one who has stoned himself into catatonia, while Freddie has stayed alert and artistic.

The thought of making out with Freddie while the others

sleep nearby is oddly arousing, as if having witnesses present for my burgeoning sexuality makes it more legitimate, even if they are unconscious. Freddie moves the guitar off the bed. I stagger over and snuggle up beside him, finding it hard to get closer with the guitar handle shoved in my face.

"Excuse me, Iris, could you move over a bit?"

"Of course," I reply, only to find that Freddie was moving the guitar not to get closer to me, but so that he could pick it up and play a folkie version of "1999." The sudden flurry of music in the room shakes everybody out of their stupor. Seth opens his eyes. He looks at me and then at Freddie. His facial muscles are either dormant or nonreactive, I can't tell. I burst into an uninspired harmony with Freddie. We sound lovely, but the sexuality of the moment is lost. And I feel kinda pissed at Freddie for not ravaging me, pissed at Seth for being such a stoner, pissed at everybody for being so relaxed while I'm so obviously tortured by factors out of my control, and really pissed I'm forced to thrust myself upon unwilling and/or terrified parties. I'm unable to obtain even minimal courtship from the opposite sex, let alone successfully break down my biobarrier. My femfence. My hoohaa hedge. My poonani portal. Jesus Christ I'm losing it.

I exit the room loudly, thumping my socks as hard as I can on the floor as I storm out. By the time I get to the end of the hallway, the tile is the cleanest it's ever been. I've figured it out. I'm just not an appealing woman, that's all. I'm too much, too moody—I mean look at me. I can't sit and smoke a joint without throwing a tantrum, I'm horrible. Who'd want such a downer? Not me.

All I can do now is close my eyes, masturbate, and figure out who turns me on more, accordingly. But I can't seem to focus on one full image for a long amount of time. I find myself alternating between large floating heads (for some reason Seth's is black and white and Freddie's is in color). Sometimes an image of Sean Connery creeps in, but in the end none of them get me going. As if a man has anything to do with my arousal level. On the contrary, the male image seems to take focus away from the actual sensation, and the only way I am able to come is if I close my eyes really hard and think of nothing, absolutely nothing but the feeling of my finger, flicking faster and faster, trying not to make too much noise under the sheets. Enveloped in the darkity of emptiness. Only then do I feel comfortable enough to experience pleasure.

I remember a large hole in my parents' bathroom wall as a child. I don't remember why my dad punched it in, but I do remember sneaking off at random times during the day to look at it, sometimes reaching up and thrusting my small hand inside, as if some gooey mystery lay in the dark cave that now existed in the plaster. Delving into the unknown gave me a cheap thrill and made the fact that my dad had an outburst emotional enough to actually create a hole in the wall a little less scary. As a child, forceful remodeling of that kind had a highly detrimental impact on me, especially during that early period of my life, which was actually a happy time of oblivion and birthday parties. We were living in a cozy apartment that had olive green carpeting and a view of the Hudson. Dad and I would play chess, while Mom made tasty Bulgarian food for the many friends that stopped by on a daily basis. Soon after the hole punch, however, I was told that my parents were splitting up, my dad was moving into a studio in the city, and my mom and I were moving into a much larger house about a mile away. Which, of course, made no sense to me whatsoever on several levels.

The hole taught me that the unexpected could happen at any moment. The fact was, it did. It does. Constantly. And it terrifies me. I try and remember that everyone has their own holes in the wall to contend with, whether they punched them in or not. But that's not always helpful when the fear that pulsates through my body is as overpowering to me as it was when I was ten.

After two weeks in Vietnam, I've come to realize that emotional stucco is harder to fix when there's no hardware store around. Whatever that means. All I know is that with every passing day I seem to shove myself further into isolation, limiting my social banter in the van to the occasional exclamation of "That's funny!" or "I need to pee." I've even stopped sticking around for Freddie's nightly folk fest. Instead, I just go sit in my room and cry, as I try to gauge how stoned everyone is by the lilt in their voice during the "hey hey hey" part of "Mrs. Robinson."

I've kept hoping that Seth will one night come up and ask me, "How are you doing?" or say, "We miss you downstairs," but none of that ever happens. Nobody comes up, not even Iris, not even once. I keep telling myself that they're just trying to let me rest. After all, my excuse is always that I'm not feeling well. (But isn't that more reason to check up on me?) To them it probably looks as if I'm just vying for attention—which is entirely accurate—but at the same time I am genuinely feeling down, and it would have been nice to have someone take an interest. Even Pappa Pat hasn't rolled in to check in on his offspring.

I know I need attention. A lot of it. I was told that quite harshly by my sixth-grade teacher, Mrs. Eisen, one afternoon after math class. Mrs. Eisen was the hippest teacher at my yeshiva, younger than the other rabbis and wives. Her long skirts were always cool, her raspy voice was rough but warmly authoritative. She was my favorite, until the day she asked me to stay behind and talk to her during recess.

"You need too much attention," she said to me, very matter-of-factly. "I can feel it—you need my approval ten times more than any other kid in class."

My stomach dropped. A nervousness overtook my body. I just liked Mrs. Eisen and wanted her to like me back. Was that not natural? Was I that different from everyone else?

"Do your parents give you attention?" she asked me.

"I think so," I replied.

"What is it then?"

"I don't know. I'm sorry."

"Is everything okay at home?" she asked.

"Daddy lives with his girlfriend and Mommy sleeps a lot. She fainted once on the floor."

I didn't even realize what I was saying, since it was the first time I had actually verbalized what was going on at home. Mrs. Eisen was silent for a moment. This was not the answer she'd been expecting.

"Your parents are getting a divorce?"

"Yes."

The expression on Mrs. Eisen's face went from factual to compassionate.

"I had no idea," she said, grabbing me in a very intense hug. That was the trigger. I started sob, sob, sobbing like I didn't know a sixth-grader could.

"It must be very hard for you," she said.

Nobody else's parents in class were divorced, and nobody besides Annie Gordon's parents knew what mine were going through. The only reason they knew was because I was carted over to sleep at Annie's house several times when things got especially sticky.

"You're not getting enough love at home, are you?" asked Mrs. Eisen.

I had no idea how to answer that. It's not like I had any gauge of comparison. Unbeknownst to me, I was just struggling to be of some stability to everyone, exhibiting remarkable composure. I'd say I was resilient, but considering the recourse that that whole period has had on my life, it's clear that my so-called resilience was temporary, a short-term survival mechanism that only delayed and even amplified the harmful effects of those past events on my present level of functioning.

At the time, my ten-year-old brain was just beginning to process the trauma I was undergoing. Mrs. Eisen's question was the first time I was actually allowed to feel the pain of the goings-on at home.

Several minutes of childlike contemplation later, I still didn't know how to answer her question. I mean the only thing my parents kept telling me throughout all the crap and the drama, the only thing they thought would make everything okay for me was "We both love you very much."

Well, maybe they did, but not enough to take me through that hellish period without my wanting extra kudos on acing my Talmud exam.

The hug was still in progress. I was afraid recess would end and everyone would find me in a pathetic crying embrace.

"Anytime you want to talk, you just let me know. I wish I would have known sooner."

And here I was, revealed. Divorce or no divorce, I was a needy, approval-seeking freak who wasn't as good as the other kids in my class.

Maybe that's when my super-self-consciousness was born. You know, the one that's plaguing me at this very moment. A hypervigilance of sorts, afraid that my behavior might be misconstrued or defined as a hindrance to others. The last thing a ten-year-old needs is self-awareness. The last thing a twenty-year-old needs is self-awareness.

And so my mind is going a mile a minute analyzing every single moment that goes by when I'm not the center of love and attention, and it's killing me. Why can't I just fucking relax?

If only I didn't feel so alone. Even the worms have left my body. I miss them, the little ones. After my last few bowel movements, I've turned and looked at my by-product in hope that a stray wormie got lost and saved himself from the medication monster, but no such luck.

They're better off living elsewhere. Not in my sorry shit.

Chapter Nineteen

Today I'm the last one to board the van, my usual seat left vacant for me. I don't mind. Everyone is too post-baked to socialize, except the Oslo Girls, who I still suspect spend their nights under a heat lamp spreading bronzing cream on each other. They are currently chirping through "Human Behavior," managing to massacre my most beloved of Björk's hits.

But no matter. The countryside is magnificent. Vast green rice fields that go on for ever, the occasional triangle hat bobbing up and down on the horizon. What a majestic, magical, poetic, filmic, inspiring sight to behold.

"This is shit."

I turn around. It's Haifa Goodfella #1. He looks mighty unhappy. "China's so much fucking greener than this."

"Shut up, man. Who cares how green China is? We're not *in* China," Seth says, truly pissed for the first time ever. And I mean *ever*.

"Yeah, be quiet," Iris chimes in.

"No, I'm serious. You guys should definitely go to China after this, Nam is a waste of time."

Pat's focusing intently on the road. I turn back around, my euphoric mental travelogue shattered by Goodfella's nonuseful honesty. Pat does not utter a word.

"Wow, look at this village!" I burst out, hoping to distract him from the horrible Israeli quality of fucktact. It works. He smiles. My enthusiasm is actually real—this tiny village is nothing less than perfect. One general store and some other little shacks that house cobblers and bicycle fixers and such. I motion to Pat to pull over.

"Pat, you want anything?" I ask.

Pat smiles. "Lemon drink, please."

I hop out of the van. The others follow. Like giddy schoolchildren we instantly become engrossed in purchasing goodies. We're in the store for about ten minutes. When we come out, my mouth drops.

The *entire village* has amassed right outside. About a hundred people are standing there in complete silence, staring at us as if we just parked our UFO. For many of these younger villagers we're the first white people they've ever seen in the flesh, which makes sense. After all, travel to these parts is, and has been, strictly restricted by the government, and we might very well be the first group of backpackers to actually stop here.

A young girl comes over and pulls on my shirt. That breaks the ice, and a second later the Goodfellas are out with their cameras. What a joy to be someone's discovery, to cause such excitement. Like a Jew in the South, but with a happy ending.

The best part about this whole frenzied anthro lovefest is that it is not agenda-driven. These villagers don't want money, they don't have souvenirs to sell or pockets to pick. They just want contact. Physical contact.

And that's what we provided. Seth demonstrated hackeysack to a young sprout, I let an old woman brush my hair, the Goodfellas danced with some teenage girls and Pat stood by the van like a proud patriarch watching his war-ring tribal sons play together at long last.

This pit stop has essentially saved me from a downward spiral into self-indulgent pitydom. More than that, I've attained a certain peacefulness, having focused my attention outward for a brief moment. I'm in Vietnam for Chrissake, and for the past few days have done nothing but focus on two men. Mere mortals, fantastic as they may be. I am in Vietnam. And *this* is what I'm going to remember, these soft faces, this utter amazement at my very presence.

Our next stop is Hoi An, a magical town full of French nostalgia with a Vietnamese twist. I spend the whole day walking around alone, away from the group, not in a "Hey, look at me" or "Hey, I don't like people," but in a "Hey, I want to focus on the sights and sounds and smells without any distractions." And what a wondrous day it is.

I've seen numerous homes and tiny alleyways, scarfed down three baguettes, and have failed to notice how dark it has gotten. The crew is probably wondering where the hell I am. Or not. It doesn't really matter. I feel satisfied, as if in a single day I had inhaled the whole country, its people and its history.

I'm in such a good mood as I enter our hotel, I don't even get annoyed at the sound of Freddie's voice singing "Brown-Eyed Girl" for the millionth time. With a big smile pasted on my face, I float past the perplexed group and ascend the stairs to my room, satisfied with my ability to still surprise people, myself included.

Halfway up the stairs I hear the sound of socked Tevas.

"Iris."

I turn around. Seth curls some hair behind his ear, girlie-style.

"Is everything okay?" he asks, concerned.

Why is my tranquility translated as an aberration, God-damit? Did they ask Buddha if *he* was just bummed?

"Everything's great. Why?"

"I don't know, you seemed distant."

"Just taking it all in, Seth."

"Oh. Gotcha. Well, you should join us later."

"Maybe I will."

I continue up the stairs, a feeling of power surging through my body. And to finish off an already perfect day, when I go to take a dump I see a string. A small string, but he is moving and has a newborn perk in his step. That's right. The worms are back. I knew they wouldn't let me down.

But all long-lost friends come with some baggage, and my bowel movement turns out to be somewhat painful—and even worse, one that offers no relief. I anxiously await a follow-up movement. It fails to arrive until eight A.M. the next morning, and by the time I'm done, I'm forty-five minutes late for our scheduled departure time. In a panic, I race out of the hotel with my rucksack slung over my shoulder haphazardly.

The whole van is waiting for me. I board it with a pained look on my face.

"Worms back, huh?" Seth says knowingly.

"Yep."

I announce it to the van. "WORMS ARE BACK!"

Everyone applauds, as if the worms were just flown in from Entebbe.

An hour into our drive, the van stops. I look at Pat,

confused. But he is staring straight ahead. I think I spot a tear in his eye. He takes a deep breath and turns around to speak to the group.

"Hello, friends. This is end of the road. I no go more north, is dangerous and uncomfortable for me. This is the end. If I get close to Hanoi, police give me trouble. This is it. It is over. I had good time, you be careful. This is the finish. No more time for me with group, no more time to spend together as your guide. It is over. This is end of trip with Pat."

The group waits a beat to see if Pat has any additional forms of expressing his message. He does.

"This is good-bye, my friends."

I want to cry. I've become truly attached to this bizarre uncle figure. I give him a big hug in the front seat. The group bursts out with perfunctory invitations to "Come to Israel," "See you in Santa Cruz," "Catch you in London, mate." Oslo refrains from making such polite gestures, which, albeit rude, is definitely a more realistic choice. Nobody really expects Pat to traverse the fjords when even Hanoi is a stretch.

"This is train station. You take train to Hanoi. Good-bye."

And with that we are dumped off and Pat races away back to Ho Chi Minh City.

Like an orphaned family ejected out of their final foster home, the group bustles sadly over to the ticket window. The smushy underage ticket sales representative informs us that there is "No cheap seat left to Hanoi. First class only. Is fifty-dollah ticket. Two ticket left. Next train only tomorrow."

My feelings of empowerment from last night are somehow still with me, and I step right up to the counter and buy a ticket. I hear a gasp from behind. Iris is in shock. Pretty aggressive move on my part. I mean I've just stepped away from her and broken a month-long traveling partnership within seconds. Well, not really. I mean we can still meet in Hanoi, but I guess my move could be interpreted as a break-away, inconsiderate of the group's needs, overassertive of my individuality, that kind of thing.

Yep, I've completely fucked up the equilibrium of the group and can feel their animosity pierce my back. I'm afraid to turn around and encounter the collective glare. But it must be done. I have my ticket and now it's time to turn around and say good-bye.

Freddie is right behind me, towering. Will he slap me or be nice enough to give me a good-bye kiss? He does neither.

"I'd like to purchase the other ticket, please."

Whoa. Was not expecting that one. I step out of the way with a smile and let him purchase his ticket. I await the double gasp from the crowd, but in vain. I guess they're still reeling from my rebellious decision to depart.

Iris catches my eye and stabs it. I've just taken her John Denver away. A double sin.

Our good-byes are cold, uncomfortable, and short. Freddie gets a bunch of hugs, but I'm sent off with just a nod and a "See ya around." On cue, it starts to pour. Itching to create some distance from the troops, I head out toward the train station. Freddie follows.

Yes, Freddie has decided to join me. What does this mean? What doesn't it mean? It means we've just decided to embark on a first-class train ride to Hanoi. Quite spontaneously.

A beautiful thing.

We show our bazillion-dollar tickets to the conductor on the platform and follow him to the first-class car. First class in hell maybe. There is no way the shithole we just entered is first class. There are over twenty people crammed onto eight wooden seats and a sniveling infant on the floor wrapped in some sort of tarp. Either this is karmic payback for our sociopathic departure or we've been fucked. Probably both. I thought I would only get payback in another life, when I would be reborn as an alpaca of some sort. Freddie looks more irked than I've ever seen him. He marches elegantly toward the conductor, his height, no doubt, terrifying to all.

"This ticket cost us fifty American dollars, my friend," Freddie says, his accent getting decidedly more cockneyesque.

The conductor laughs. He tells us to sit down or get off the train. At this point there is no place to even sit down. And there is definitely no way I'm standing for twelve hours.

"He wants more money," Freddie says. The look on his face tells me he's been through this a million times before.

Turns out fucknut wants a lot more money. A hundred more dollars in fact. Freddie and I both know we're being eaten alive by the bastard, but at this point we don't care. Well, at least I don't. I destroyed my friendship with an entire group of people and I better enjoy it. So we reach into our respective stashes and each hand the guy a fifty. Like magic, our tickets turn to gold, and we are led two miles down to the front end of the train, the other world, the first-class cabin.

Chapter Twenty

This is more like it. Everything in the *real* first class is up-holstered in pleasant blue colors. A family of three is already present in our car and sprawled across the bottom beds. (Vietnamese WASPs if you will, only nonwhite and Buddhist.)

This family is apparently big on citrus; there are orange rinds everywhere—on the floor, on the bed, in the kid's shoe. I guess even first-class citizenry have this misconception that rinds are somehow biodegradable in a *will decompose within minutes even if left on plush carpeting* kind of way.

Freddie hops onto the upper bunk on one side of the cabin as I elegantly climb up onto mine on the other side. There is a sea of family and fruit between us. He's changing shirts. I don't think I've ever seen anything beyond the peasant blouse, and I am pleasantly surprised, the messy fabric having successfully masked his toned physique. I'm actually feeling a stirring. Who would have thought—the perfect place to lose my virginity, atop a Vietnamese family on the way to Hanoi. What a great story to tell the grandchildren!

"Why don't you come here, Freddie? I feel like chatting . . . I'd rather not yell."

"Okay, why not."

"Why not" definitely ranks as the most passive and un-flattering response ever. Why not. How about, "Yes, I'd love to." Or an equally satisfactory, "Sounds great."

I remember a second date I had once—the guy had invited me to dinner at his place. I arrived right on time, all dressed up and excited. He, in contrast, opened the door in shorts and a T-shirt. The TV was on. And it stayed on after I sat down on the couch and after I attempted to make conversation. In short, the fucker would not stop watching television. This was our second date, for Chrissake, not our one-year anniversary.

I finally got up off the couch and stormed toward the door. I had actually managed to get all the way to the door and open it before he finally acknowledged my impending departure. Without getting up off the couch, he asked me why I was leaving.

"I don't feel like you want me to stay," I confessed.

And to that, Charmie replied: "Well . . . I don't *not* want you to stay."

It took me a minute to process this ridiculous response. I wish I had been prepared for it, so I could retort with, "I don't *not* want to *not* think you're *not* an idiot," but all I could muster was, "Yeah, well . . . yeah."

In one elegant move, Freddie succeeds in climbing atop the bed without disturbing the feety family. But that's where the elegance comes to an abrupt close. You see, these bunk beds were designed for narrow Vietnamese rich kids. So once Freddie is on the bed, an odd game of vertical Twister ensues. I squish myself against the wall, while he attempts to sit cross-legged beside me, which proves to be a very precipitous endeavor. He then hesitantly lies down, but he's still too fucking wide, and I find myself with one arm lodged in the space between the bed and the wall, my finger touching some weird hairy object below. I yank my hand back up, hitting my elbow painfully on the metal frame.

"Here. I'll sit up," I say, planning to ride Freddie like a fine cricket player. Worst-case scenario he'll throw me down on the blue carpeting. The orange rinds will pad my fall.

Freddie lies down flat. I slowly get on top of him, gently placing my legs around him but making sure to not engage in any direct crotch-to-crotch contact.

So here I am, hovering three inches above Freddie's body. My thighs feel the burn and we both feel kind of stupid. He's obviously not hard. But I also haven't done anything. I guess this is the time to lean in for a kiss. I mean he did crawl onto my bed, what did he expect—Canasta?

Landing commences. I begin to descend. Approaching lip tarmac. Fear mounting. Three. Two. One. Contact. The man kisses me back. Success! Well, sort of. I'm moving my tongue in his mouth in eager exploration, but his tongue is just lying there like Wiener schnitzel.

So I stop. Not because I want to, but because I know he wants me to. I can feel his body relax as I retract from his dormant oral cavern.

"I think I'll get a little shut-eye," he says.

"Alright," I respond, and with slightly superfluous force shove him off the bed. He almost crashes onto the floor, but at the last minute Mama Nam gets up and creates a barrier for his fall. His leg brushes her shoulder, but lucky for him, he grabs on to me before any serious impact occurs.

The rest of my journey to Hanoi is spent watching everyone sleep. My dreams of erotic adventures on the top bunk of a Vietnamese train are fulfilled by my index finger. Surprise, surprise. Never thought the smell of oranges could be so sexy.

Freddie and I checked into a lovely hotel, one of ten or so in Hanoi. Interesting, this plethora of hotels, considering this is the Commie part of the country.

Things have changed since we arrived. For one thing, Freddie is dead. It's Brian now, per his request. He's turning more proper English with each passing minute, perhaps prepping himself for his return home. I don't mind. I kind of like being on a truly first-name basis with him, a renewal of sorts.

These last few days in Hanoi have been very peaceful. I've found new joy in spending time with one person. Iris and the others are a mere blur in my mind. It's just me and Brian taking moonlit walks around the city lake, riding our rented bicycles to quaint little corners of town (like the café in that Catherine Deneuve movie), purchasing silk and other local goods.

Yes, indeed, my time here could not be more enjoyable—or less sexual. In short, we sleep as siblings. Maybe my sibling is gay. Despite the fact that he goes on and on about Fiona, his ex-girlfriend whom he lived with in Kuala Lumpur. As Brian tells it, Fiona was very ill for a long time, during which he tended to her every need and desire, but Fi was an ungrateful bitch to him, using him for everything he had, all his goodness and givingness, before taking a big worm shit on him, blah blah blah.

But I'm not complaining. Not at all. The lack of sexual pressure and expectation has actually allowed me to enjoy the city in a tranquil and fulfilling fashion, without my mind racing a mile a minute wondering who's thinking what and what underwear do I have on and oh shit will there be K-Y at the local kiosk, etc., etc. Perhaps my intensive bout of unsuccessful attempts has also drained me, not of hope, but of energy to try. Either way I'm feeling more relaxed than I have in a long time.

Tonight I've decided to get cultural and pick up some tickets to a water puppet show, a Lonely Planet "Must See." Brian and I are both eager for some theatricality and a formal night out, Western-world style.

I put on my clean pants and shine my flip-flops, Brian deigns to wash *and* comb his hair, and we venture off on our bikes to the theater.

Front-row seats. A chic Vietnamese crowd surrounds us. In the center of the stage is a large pool full of dark, dirty water. In front of the pool is a musician holding an odd stringed instrument. He begins to play as the lights go down, producing the most disturbing, horrifying sound imaginable. If I made those sounds for you right now, you'd smack me in seconds.

Pluck, pluck, pluck, cringe, cringe, cringe.

Silence.

Blackout.

Lights up.

Out of the depths of the pool massive puppets emerge, gliding with much effort through the sewage. Their movement grows into a frenzied puppet orgy as the dragon heads gyrate faster and faster, the violin on crack screaming louder and louder.

Brian has a lemon-up-the-butt grimace. He looks at me in horror. I stifle a laugh as the graceless musician looks up, detecting imminent mockery. Front rows suck.

Lucky for our sanity, the show is less than an hour long. We're both exhausted, however, having undergone such a dissonant ordeal. I can't get the damn screeching plucking sound out of my head; in fact, I haven't stopped making the sound since we got on our bikes. Good Lord, Brian is making it too. *Creeowwwwowowopluckpluck.* I increase my volume. He increases his. With ridiculous grins on our faces we commence a freakish top-of-our lungs screech fest that manages to disturb even the most oblivious locals speeding past us. I do not resist the urge and begin to harmonize a half step down Brian's D-flat screech. He pulls over abruptly.

"Sorry, Brian, I didn't mean to mock harmonizing. I was just playing."

Brian just looks at me. His face is soft, but he's not smiling. I don't think he's ever not smiled at me before. Come to think of it, he's been smiling nonstop from the minute I met him. But not now. Now he's just looking at me, not angry, just serious. It feels weird. I don't know how to handle it. So I smile. But the smile feels inappropriate, so I wipe it off and avert my gaze to avoid direct eye contact.

"We part ways tomorrow, Iris."

I had forgotten that. He to London, me back to Bangkok. Tomorrow. Yes. My stomach. Again that visceral response. Abandonment is a natural part of backpacking as each member goes their separate ways, but for me it has always signified something a lot darker, a lot more depressing.

I lean over and give Brian a hug without getting off my bike, almost crushing his testicles with my handlebars in the process.

"It was very special, spending time with you, Iris."

It gets very quiet. The air is still, the drone of the surrounding bicycles disappears. A strange romantic moment that neither of us want to spoil with sexual action. I feel oddly older right now.

My first real connection. Untainted by agenda, able to thrive thanks to this social bubble of sorts, this magical island where Brian and I were able to feel like the only people on the planet while simultaneously surrounded by multitudes of humanity.

A melancholy fills the air as we get into bed, knowing we'll probably never see each other again. I creep in first. Brian follows, lying closer to me than he ever has before. I can feel his breath on my back, and it warms every part of my body like a safety blanket. I turn around to face him. We look in each other's eyes for just a second, before shutting them in perfect unison.

Chapter Twenty-One

Here I am, back on Vietnam Air, one highly evolved
month later. I enjoy this newfound tranquility for seven
gorgeous minutes. And on the eighth, a small fabric am-
phibian rears its head from first class. Iris. She's making
her way down the aisle, clan in tow. Honest to God, I had
forgotten about them. I had entered a different, elevated
reality, one that entailed a Juliet Binoche–like experience
with an older Englishman (even taller than Jeremy Irons)
in an exotic city, while they had merely continued their
trip in the same stingy backpacker mode as before. I was
now older, more mature, and a much better person than
they were.

Iris takes her seat next to me. We don't say a word. And
that's fine with me. I'm sick of this guilt. I don't give a shit
that she's mad at me.

I also don't give a shit that the minute we arrive in Bangkok
the posse hops in a cab together. To Kao San Road, no doubt.
I jump into my own private taxi and check into a nice air-
conditioned guesthouse, one that costs up to a buck fifty more
a night, with a bathroom *inside* the room. That's right. You
heard me.

* * *

Tonight I'm feeling nostalgic and head to the one place I know will bring back good memories: the Queens Club at Phat Phong.

I enter like a regular. The girls surround me immediately. For the next few hours I tell them stories of their brave sisters up north in Chiang Mai and my special relationship with one of them in particular. In turn, they share their life stories with me, their newfound den mother.

Yes, I can see a new career path for me: guidance counselor of the Thai underworld. I'll go from club to club, helping girls curb the urge to shoot darts out of their womb, teaching them valuable life skills, assisting them in realizing their full potential. Before you know it, they'll be registering for community colleges, getting certified as computer programmers or dental assistants.

Think about it. I could do real good here, I could live with the virginity and not have to worry about losing it—it would be *part* of the job.

A hostile messenger approaches, and I am suddenly requested to purchase another drink. The owner, I'm told, feels that I'm distracting his girls from seeking profitable conquests. And so I leave my angels to their duties, my dreams of reforming the misguided put on the back burner as I am reminded who the misguided in this whole picture really is.

I exit the club back into the marketplace and return to the stall where I purchased those prize candlesticks my first night in Bangkok, in hopes of finding the matching incense holder I'd regretted not buying the first time around. It is indeed sitting there, but I just walk past without even stopping to fondle it. Suddenly it looks cheap to me. Tacky. Self-serving and inconsiderate.

Okay. You win. I've been feeling like crap about the whole

Iris thing and I've just been in complete denial. Yes, my room is nicer now, yes, my ceiling fan fucking works, but what I want is Iris's love back for my horrible, bitchy, selfish, disgusting behavior. I was part of the group, and I ignored that fact and just did what served me.

It's a particularly sticky night in Bangkok tonight, the smell of fish rinds hangs in the air, everything seems to be moving a little slower, accentuating my misery. I'm not sleepy, so I head to Thai World, which is packed to capacity. I take a seat particularly close to the television set and order my trio of banana shakes.

There's some weird shmutz on the table that I manage to scratch off with my fingernail. As I contemplate why on earth I would dare use my own fingernail for such a task, Iris walks in. I'd be lying if I told you my hand doesn't shoot up like a rocket, Ima-in-Torino style, while my voice belts out at lightning velocity and thunderous volume:

"IRIS! OVER HERE! I'M OVER HERE! COME JOIN ME!"

She looks my way with such deathly hate that I wonder if I need to call in backup. I smile sheepishly, my eyes following her as she weaves her way through the crowded tables. It's unclear whether she will indeed make her way to my table. I think she's mumbling "traitor to the guillotine" under her breath.

She is coming to my table.

She has arrived at my table.

She's still mumbling.

"Mumble mumble . . . Vietnam . . . mumble . . . train . . . mumble . . . bitch."

"Hey, stranger!" I yelp, with a smile that says, "Love me, I'm a horrible person."

"Not cool what you did, Iris."

Well, at least we're not going to beat around the bush.

"I'm sorry, Iris, I wasn't thinking."

"Really not cool."

"I'm sorry. I wasn't thinking."

"I'm really pissed at you."

"Yes, I know, I'm sorry, I wasn't thinking."

"Okay."

"I'm sorry, I wasn't thinking."

She is silent for a moment, and I wonder if she's waiting for me to say the line one more time.

"I'm sorry, I wasn't thinking."

She doesn't even blink. I guess I should've just shut up. The tension is killing me. Finally she speaks.

"Want to go to Nepal?" she asks, her face stone still.

"Yes!" I say.

"Yes!" I say again.

"Yes!" I say yet again.

Silence.

Maybe the repetition technique is working against me.

I bear this tormenting silence for a full minute before it dawns on me that she may indeed need one more. One more will bring it home.

"I'm sorry, Iris." *(Long meaningful pause, a slight squint, and a glance down at the table.)* Really, I am."

She is actually surprised at my sincerity. So am I. She cracks a faint smile, and I can tell she's relieved. I am, too.

Nepal

Chapter Twenty-Two

Ahhh Kathmandu . . . the cool, crisp Himalayan air . . . the snow . . . the temples . . . the cow shit. Quite otherworldly actually, in an odd, nonreligious kind of way. Almost like a field of wheat, where one feels spirituality not in the presence of God or some divine being, but in the very simplicity and abstract infinite nature of the place.

I feel amazingly healthy, now that I don't have the humid stench of deadcodcatrice permeating my pores at all times. A hot shower here actually succeeds in leaving me with a clean feeling that lasts longer than five minutes. I seem to have an appetite that is not worm-related, my cheeks are rosy and my skin is glowing. *Let's trek!*

Since neither I nor Iris are what one would call North Face poster girls, we're somewhat limited on our choices of trek. Meaning Mount Everest is not really an option, not by a long shot. And so we head to Pokhara, a base departure point for many of the "lighter" treks.

Trek prep is not as easy as it sounds, at least from an administrative point of view. Before we can go anywhere we have to obtain a trekking permit, as in permit office and permit man and waiting on a long-ass line to have your passport stamped with a permit stamp, all for a mysterious permitty fee of forty dollars.

If there is any upside to this bureaucratic sludgefest, it is that there are two hot Israeli guys waiting right behind us in line. And I thought I was over the whole man thing. Not a chance. Not with these fine specimens shoved in my face by the Almighty up above.

Specimen One: A tall, handsome muscular man with a shaved head and perfect goatee (not the lame kind that doesn't connect around the lips or the super-hairy kind that hints to fuzzy backs and buttocks), oval smart-guy glasses, behind which sit somewhat beady yet nonetheless appealing green eyes, and a great, *great* ass.

Specimen Two: A lean, artsy Goa hippie with long brown hair, a pointier beatnik goatee, and huge warm brown eyes that emanate both wit and intellect.

These guys are the rare dreamy hybrid of #3s and #6s—weathered, cool, *and* smart-looking. Androgynous Iris fails to notice the choice merchandise, so I deign to get their attention in my usual witty manner.

"This is a charade organized by the Nepalese government!" I yell in mock protest.

They turn my way but continue talking, their interest visibly piqued. I proceed.

"They couldn't care less if I sold crack on top of Everest, they just want my forty bucks."

The specimens laugh. I turn around coyly. The shaven-headed one catches my eye first. Target A.

Turns out his name is Yotam. The other's Udi. They are an enticing duo up until the moment they're joined by a gorgeous girl named Nili. She's got that gross "natural" kind of beauty: flawless skin, seductive chestnut eyes, smooth black hair, and a stunning body that's obvious even under the heavy parka and sweatpants she's wearing. She is, in fact, the perfected version of me, every flaw of mine miraculously corrected. It's nice to discover you were a practice run for a much better version yet to come.

Her arrival sucks everyone's attention away from me, leaving me no choice but to turn back around midsentence. Hey, I'm not about to waste energy on a couple of lost cases. They're obviously infatuated with her, especially Yotam, whose heart rate increased the minute she came into view. I could hear it, Poe style.

Iris continues to chat with them, and I feel a pang of annoyance at her lack of loyalty. Read my mind, woman.

"What trek are you girls gonna take?" Yotam asks her.

"Uh, I don't know, we haven't decided yet. Something light and easy," Iris says.

Great, now they think I'm a cardiac patient. Or even worse, as old as she is—a geriatric twenty-six.

"I wouldn't mind easy myself," Yotam replies. "Fifteen years of smoking does that to you. We're thinking of doing the Poonhill, it's only a week long and it's supposed to be pretty easy. Our other friends, Kushnir and Shimi, are back at the guesthouse looking into it."

"Sounds great," Iris says. "What do you think, Iris, do you want to do the Poonhill, too?" she asks, finally turning back to face me.

For the first time, she has proven to be shrewd in the ways of getting me laid.

"Sure," I say, turning back around to find the boys smiling and Nili glaring at me like I peed on her boypatch. Nonetheless, we're in. We have agreed to join the clan on their trek to Poonhill and also on a bonus white-water rafting trip beforehand.

We have plenty of time to get acquainted with our new

trek mates before we reach the permit counter. The entire afternoon, it turns out. During which time the two other members of Yotam's traveling party join us; one is Silent Shimi, Nili's chaperone of sorts (who might as well have a leash around him the way he's groveling at his Master's feet), and the other's Kushnir, a freckled, goofy-looking, string-beany man whose class clown presence seems to put everyone in a good mood instantly. His warm hug only strengthens my sense he'll be a joyful addition to the journey.

Iris and Nili have been hitting it off famously, which I'm perfectly fine with since it gives me time to charm the boys and learn more about the specific nature of their relationship with Threatbitch. I decide to go with the coyly aggressive approach, and wait for a moment when Yotam looks at Nili for a second longer than friendship would indicate.

"How long have you guys been together?" I ask.

Nili looks at my forehead, then giggles and whispers something to Yotam, who giggles in turn.

"We're best friends," she says, making goo-goo eyes at him in the process.

"Oh," I reply, trying my best to not show relief or slap her cheek with my passport.

The "white water" we are rafting on is a slow-moving mass of sludge, drudge, and other dges that I can't seem to name right now. I blame the massive joint I've been given. And thank God for it. It's enabled me to shoot the shit with the guys without focusing on Nili's whiny voice or the various violent impulses that arise within me with her every utterance.

In essence, Nili is the only thing standing in the way of me jumping Yotam's bones. He's definitely the one I want. It's not that Udi isn't hot—there's just something about him that's annoying. Like the fact that he's currently sitting next to me by the bonfire and won't shut up. And while Udi is definitely more intelligent than Yotam, he also has that way about him that screams *I'm well-read and full of knowledge. But I'm also really annoying, which is why I make such an effort to be so well-read and full of knowledge. I'm hoping my brilliance and goatee will distract girls from my annoyingess and get me laid. It hasn't worked so far, but I'm still trying.*

I wish Yotam were sitting here instead. I'm sure he'd let me talk more. I'm kind of surprised he isn't, since I really thought I gained some ground with him on the raft today while Nili was napping. But the minute we parked, bitch came back to life and the two of them went off to have some heart-to-heart in the bushes.

Iris has assured me nothing is going on between them (she and Nili have already become full-on confidantes), but I still have the feeling that Yotam has the hots for her. And why not? She's hot. Plus, she's not bright enough to be threatening, and not dumb enough to turn a smart guy off. I guess "smart enough to fuck" would be the correct term. Actually "smart enough to fuck on a regular basis" would be more accurate. Okay, fine. "Smart enough to fuck, marry, and worship till the end of time." Happy?

Iris, Shimi, and Kushnir are out cold, and I'm losing patience with Udi's anecdotes. He's currently elaborating on how Amsterdamian hash-curing techniques have evolved since 1986.

"Are you okay?" he suddenly asks.

Oops. I didn't realize my face was scrunched up in an expression of agony.

"What? Oh yes, I'm fine."

He leans in for a kiss, and I don't resist, knowing full well it's the only way he'll shut up.

He is a horrible, horrible kisser. An enthused boa constrictor down my throat, all drool and roast beef tongue.

As I struggle to keep my windpipe open, I get the creepy feeling that this kiss has now sealed my fate. Udi and I are now "involved." Yotam is suddenly out, Udi is in, and it's all my fault.

Chapter Twenty-Three

Day one of Poonhill. The only thing that keeps me from leaping off the mountain in shame at my lack of stamina is the fact that Iris is in even worse shape than I am, and is always an hour or so behind us, escorted by her two sherpas.

Hey, let's be honest here. We all have sherpas carrying our packs. That's the Israeli way. Three years of military is enough to make even the most avid trekker a lazy ass. Not that I spent my army time lugging the wounded to safety. But still, there's absolutely no reason to suffer needlessly, that's our parents' job.

These sherpas are just as astounding as the scenery, the way they prance up the trail barefoot, carting three, sometimes even four rucksacks on their backs, as if they were lumps of cotton candy.

Other nationalities look down upon the use of sherpas. We've already run across some Danes and Aussies along the trail, all sherpa free. For what? To prove you can carry heavy shit? Stop trying to be so independent in the wilderness, what good does that do anyone? None. Especially the poor sherpie you're depriving of a steady income.

Meanwhile, Udi's behavior is nothing short of terrifying. He is by far the most caring, sensitive, kind man I've ever met. He will not leave my side, offering his hand at every turn, literally wanting to carry me up the mountain. It's disgusting.

Theory A: If I were really into him, his kindness would only make me want him more.

Theory B: His kindness is what's preventing me from wanting him.

Theory B, of course, implies that I'm way more fucked up than even I imagined.

The fact is I've turned into an annoyed bitch. The sweeter he gets, the colder I become. It's a convenient and affordable way to force someone out of their nice-cave and into a black hole of resentment and hatred. But I shan't be too hard on myself, for just as I have my thing of being bitchy to the nice guy, Udi has his thing of being nice to the bitch. A horrific combination nevertheless. Two pathetic souls, combined to form a sado-maso machine of reciprocated tender abuse.

The first day of trekking was ten hours long and by the time Udi and I get to the guestshack, the rest of the clan (sans Iris) is already enjoying hot chocolate and marijuana.

Just in case everyone was not aware we were "involved," Udi grabs my hand right before we enter the shack, to ensure proper information proliferation. I order a hot chocolate from the lady shack owner who smiles and promptly disappears out some back door.

Three hours later she has yet to return. Where could she have gone? The only thing outside is snow. It's not like she could've hopped over to the neighbors ten thousand feet below to borrow some sugar.

Luckily, Udi is in the corner rolling a joint with both

hands, thereby temporarily liberating mine from his touch. Prissy Nili doesn't smoke, and neither does Iris, so the two of them have removed themselves from the smoking circle and gone off to write poetry together.

Yotam is sitting awfully close to me on the sofa. "This pot is strong," he says to nobody in particular, whereupon he abruptly stretches out and lays his head on my lap. This is odd. Good, but odd. I look over at Udi nervously. He smiles widely. I guess he has no problem with the seating arrangement.

Yotam's head nestles deeper into my thigh. He must be staring right up my nostrils. I look down. It's hard to make real eye contact with him through his glasses. Something about the light reflection at this angle.

"Come here, I want to tell you something," he says mischievously.

"What?"

"Come here, I can't say it out loud."

I look at Udi awkwardly once again. He's deep in budding concentration. Coast clear.

I lean down sloppily. My ear touches Yotam's lips. I literally go wet at the touch. The sexual energy between us is insane.

"You look really beautiful right now," he whispers, managing to lightly brush my earlobe with his tongue in the process.

"Thank you."

"Kiss me," he says.

Okay, now this is really getting weird. Udi is right there—Oh wait, he's gone. I guess he went to the bathroom for a minute.

Let's think about this. We all know what I really want to

do. And in reality, Yotam is the best friend here, not me. What conscience do I need to exercise in this situation? For all I know these guys share girls all the time. Otherwise Yotam wouldn't be doing this, right?

Thank God for sound logical reasoning.

I take the plunge and lean down, the angle much more conducive to kissing then conversation.

Yotam is a phenomenal kisser. Soft lips, gentle tongue. No roast beef on rye here, just probing yumminess. We are suddenly interrupted by a voice from the back.

"Your hot chocolate is here."

I look up. Udi is staring at us with a huge smile frozen on his face. Could it be to hide the pain of betrayal and ego-stompage? I take the hot chocolate from off the table and sip it as if God were funneling it into my soul for salvation.

I manage to scorch the bottom half of my esophagus. Holding back tears of heat and embarrassment, I mutter, "I think I might go to bed now," gently removing Yotam's head from my lap, before scurrying out the door. Give them time to work it out, I tell myself. They need to discuss this, discuss me, discuss how we work this out. Cuz I don't want to be with Udi anymore, I never have. And Yotam is now a possibility, a reality. At least I hope so. Yotam is the best friend here, not me. Not me.

The bed is cold. My body is tired. Drama has taken its toll on me, not to mention all that hand holding. And the trek was hard, too. I am asleep in seconds, my fatigue outweighing my angst for a change. I am awakened by the door opening. A gust of snowy air penetrates the room.

"Hi."

It's Yotam. His hand touches my cheek and he sits down next to me.

"Is everything okay with you two?" I ask, bringing his hand back to my face.

"Don't worry about a thing. It's fine."

"You sure? Udi is cool with this?"

"He's my best friend, he wants the best for me."

I'm about to ask him if Nili is what's best for him, but I opt to shut up. Instead, I pull him down and we engage in a passionate kiss. A kiss that extends to us both lying naked, and me garnering enough courage to brush his penis lightly with the back of my hand.

Where the hell were you four days ago, my man? Where?!

Chapter Twenty-Four

Ah. Day one with my new man. What a difference between Udi and Yotam. No more unnecessary coddling. Here's a man who not only refuses to hold my hand, but one who walks two steps ahead of me in complete obliviousness. Here's a man I can relate to and respect. A man I can reveal my clingy side to—a side he doesn't mind, it seems. Maybe because he doesn't really acknowledge it, allowing it to drift off the mountain into the atmosphere.

My newfound joy has not been supported by the group, who have given me the complete cold shoulder, Iris included. Unbelievable—while Yotam is still Mr. Popular, I've been dubbed Satan's hooker. You'd think I smeared myself with baby oil and slid off of Udi right onto Yotam's cock. What horror stories are being spread around? Is Nili the culprit?

The important thing is Yotam is into me. My animal attraction to him is overwhelming and brings me great hope and joy for the future. After all, he jeopardized his friendship with his best friend to be with me, that's got to mean something! He's wanted me from the minute he met me. I know it. I dream it. I wish it. I imagine it. I fabricate it.

* * *

So far, sex with Yotam has been logistically impossible; during the day there's neither time nor space along the narrow, snowy mountain trails, while at night we've been sharing a large room with the rest of the group. (Yotam would probably have no problem fucking with forty people around, but even he seems to comprehend the sensitivity of the situation.)

Tomorrow morning is the peak event of our journey: the ascent of Poonhill Mountain. The custom on this trek is to get up two hours before dawn, climb the mountain, and watch the sunrise from its peak. That's why people take this trek, and it's supposed to be incredible.

Spirits are high in anticipation of the big day, and we spend the night dancing in a frenzy, smoking like mad, the hot chocolate flowing like milk from Lucifer's bosom. With Poonhill beckoning, nothing can bring us down, not even me.

It's 4:30 in the morning, and I'm surprised to find I'm the only one ready to go. Yotam is unwakeable. Iris mumbles that her back hurts. The others are too stoned-over to suck up their drool off the pillow. And Udi . . . well, I heard him scuttle out over two hours ago. He's probably halfway up the mountain by now.

It's just me then, all geared up and ready to view the beautiful sunrise while these morons sleep the goal-filled morning away. So be it. I need to be alone. I haven't been alone in days. Weeks. Shit, *months*. Since that first morning in Vietnam, I haven't spent more than a brief bathroom visit by myself. This solo climb may be the perfect opportunity to gather my thoughts and figure out what's wrong with me this week.

The crisp air pierces my psychopathologies like a knife.

It's too cold and pure for them up here, and they dissipate with every strenuous step farther up the mountain, the altitude utterly intoxicating. As I ascend, I'm surrounded by clouds so thick the trail is barely visible. How on earth am I supposed to see the sunrise if I'm engulfed by clouds?

Somebody's coming down the trail. I recognize the wide, manic steps. It's Udi. Great. Confrontation is weird any time, any place, but it's much worse on a snowy mountain trail at five in the morning. But I can deal. We're both adults. What's the worst that can happen—He'll shove me off the mountain?

It's so cloudy that we don't enter each other's view until Udi is a foot away from me. We both stand there, hiding behind our sunglasses.

"How was it up there?" I ask, my fake-friendly voice only amplified by the rarefied atmosphere.

"You can't see shit."

I laugh with gusto. Contrary to both my desire and instinct, I attempt to generate more conversation, hoping that it will somehow get us to a point where it's all natural and safe and great and he won't hate me anymore and I'll get that icky feeling out of my stomach for good.

"So I guess there's no point in me going up there, huh?" I say, maintaining a light chuckle in my voice.

"Not really." He says flatly.

"I guess I'll go back then."

Udi says nothing to this and turns around to continue his descent. So much for normalization. No way in hell I can apologize right now. It would seem too ridiculous. More than that, I fear he'd embark on a passionate verbalization of all the horrible things I already know about myself, only giving them the added sting of external confirmation.

So I let him walk on for a few seconds before slowly beginning my descent behind him. Dammit. I don't want to deal with this anymore. When am I going to be happy? Don't I deserve to be happy? Why does guilt have to factor into *every* fucking little thing I do that's good for me? I wanted Yotam, he made a move, I cooperated. Jesus fucking Christ, I get angry just thinking about it. Yotam was the one who made a move—Him. Not me. Him. *Not me!*

"NOT ME!"

Udi stops.

"Did you say something?"

Oh shit, I did just say something.

"What? No, nothing."

"Oh."

He keeps walking. His gait has softened a touch. His shoulders seem more relaxed. Maybe he doesn't think I'm a horrible person. A slut perhaps, but not a horrible person.

He's slowing down. (So I can catch up?) I take the hint and pick up my pace. Soon we are walking together, and I can feel my stomach pit slightly shrink to honeydew size.

"Where is everybody anyway?" he asks.

"In bed."

"Of course! What was I thinking?"

We share a laugh, a real one this time.

I still want to bring it up, but I don't. He's gotten over me. He must have. I mean come on, I'm not that hard to get over. Maybe he really didn't care in the first place and I was just upset over nothing. For all I know he's fucking Nili on the side.

Being nice to someone who treated you like shit can only mean one of two things: you have no self-respect and your backbone is made of industrial-strength Pathetic, or you just don't give a shit about the person who hurt you. Since I don't buy that you can really "not give a shit" about someone who grossly mistreated you, I can only assume the former; that making peace with that person is a pathetic act that just shows one's lack of spine and sorry existence.

My father had clearly once been of my school of thought, harboring bitter anger toward my mother for events that predated my birth, even citing them as reason for his consequent misconduct. Once our entire family unit exploded, his Toxic Resentment Belief System™ was bequeathed to me in an honorary ceremony on the steps of the MOMA. (The turnout was quite impressive, even former mayor Koch was in attendance.)

After that momentous event, every time I was passed over to my dad for the day, my parents would kiss each other on the cheek. I could feel my blood rise. "How could you even say hello to one another!" I would exclaim, civil behavior between the two of them seeming grossly unnatural and disturbing to me. "If you had any self-respect, mom, you'd be mean to him until the end of time!"

They eventually became very good friends. Which, of course, annoyed the shit out of me. It was as if their being friends made light of the trauma I underwent due to their time as enemies. If you were going to be friends, than why the hell couldn't you have done that *before* all that shit hit the fan? You could have spared me a lot of grief, not to mention numerous sticky issues that obviously still plague me on a daily basis.

But my theory on such matters seems to be crumbling. For here is Udi treating me with respect, and I don't feel like he's pathetic or has no backbone. Not even close. He seems classy, mature, a bigger man. A better person. A forgiving soul. Or just a highly convincing actor.

By the time we get back to the cabin, the gang is all up and ready to go. Home, that is. Nobody wants to trek up Poonhill, and it's decided that we'll just head back to Pokhara. I look for Yotam, but he's not in the room. I refrain from asking about his whereabouts aloud, lest it taint my newfound truce with Udi.

So I head back to the room to pack. When I open the door, I find Yotam and Nili on my bed playing cards. She looks up at me as I enter, a whorey glaze in her eyes. She giggles, as is her habit. Yotam giggles in turn, giving me a brief "hey" before returning to his hand.

I pack swiftly and wait outside, finding more comfort in the freezing air than watching Bonnie and Clyde flirt over a game of Go Fish.

Chapter Twenty-Five

The final day of the trek is supposed to be the most torturous, involving no less than a full-day nonstop descent that kills the knees and mangles the soul. Speaking of which, Yotam and I are on a break from each other today. (He informed me an hour ago that he'd been neglecting his friends and would rather walk with them for a change. I, in turn, feigned support and prepared for a long, lonely day.) To my surprise, however, Stringbean Kushnir joins me upon my descent. In fact, he doesn't leave my side the whole way down. I somehow feel undeserving of his kindness, as if even associating with me were a mitzvah.

He waits about twenty seconds into our walk before bringing up the kaka.

"Feel like shit, don't you?"

I can tell he isn't judging me—just being honest. It's refreshing.

"Yes, I've felt like shit from the moment it happened."

"I can understand that. Bad move on your part."

"Hey, I'm not the one with the best friend."

"That's the thing, Iris, *they're* best friends, you're just a passing fancy. Of course they're going to get over it. And you're the one who's going to suffer."

"But why should I have the conscience? He made the move on me!"

"I know, but Udi was fawning over you hand and foot, what about *his* feelings?"

"What about *my* feelings, Kushnir?"

"You're not that selfish, I know you're not. Otherwise you wouldn't feel this shitty. I'm just telling you the truth. People will judge you because you're the woman. Udi liked you and you hurt his feelings. The fact that Yotam was a shitty friend is not as interesting to people, they'd rather blame you. Even Udi would rather blame you, because he would hate to think his best friend is a shit."

"I know, I know. I'm just frustrated. I always feel guilty whenever I do something that's good for me."

"The question is, what's good for you?"

"I don't know. I know I wanted to be with Yotam."

"Are you happy now?"

"I guess I thought it would all just work out. I didn't think Udi liked me that much."

"Why not?"

"Why would he? I'm so fucked up, everybody hates me."

Kushnir stops at this, trying to see if I'm being sincere. When he decides that I am, he takes me by the shoulders and looks down at me. Literally, he's over a foot taller than I am.

"You're an incredible person, Iris. You make everyone laugh, you're pretty and sexy and funny and smart, why wouldn't he want you? We all want you."

"But I'm a horrible person," I say, having a very hard time believing him and feeling a deluge of tears coming on.

"No, you're not a horrible person, you just made a mistake and you worry about it too much."

"Do you want to sleep with Nili, too?"

"What? Where the hell did that come from?"

"I don't know. I can't stand her, I'm sorry."

"Why? She's such a sweetheart!" he exclaims, genuinely perplexed at my feelings of animosity. Dammit, Kushnir, you were doing so well. Why do you have to be such a blind putz like all the other men who think any bitch who's beautiful is a "sweetheart." Why can only us quirky girls see the truth? Why? Why?

"Well, I have nothing against her," I lie. "She . . . she just doesn't like me."

"Why do you think that?" he persists, the look in his eye increasingly more vacant as his penis nibbles further away at his frontal lobe, devouring any remnants of wisdom and insight that were displayed earlier.

He honestly has no idea what I'm talking about. A lost cause. I just have to remember what he said before the annoying stuff. How *everyone* wants *me*. I mean, let's face it. He didn't call Nili funny and sexy, he just said she was a sweetheart. Nevertheless, before he has the chance to list her many other virtues, I steer the conversation in a more agreeable direction—silence.

We've all reunited at the end of the trail and just boarded the bus back to Pokhara. Are Yotam and I still together? I have no fucking idea. He sat next to Nili without even asking me first. What does that mean?

Iris sits beside me, listening to her meditative water tape. I have the sudden urge to lay my head on her shoulder, feeling an increased comfort in her presence. I lean my head on the dirty window instead, letting it fall with a melancholic thud.

"Are you feeling okay?" she asks.

"Yeah, I'm fine."

That seems to satisfy her, and she changes her tone from caring to logistical.

"I've been talking to Udi and Yotam."

"I'm sure they had wonderful things to say about me."

Iris doesn't respond to this sardonic comment. Even a half-assed "Oh, don't be silly" would have been in order. But we move on.

"They want to go on safari, do you?" she asks, a lovely taupe shade to her offer.

"Do you want me to come?" ("I don't *not* want you to come . . .")

"Why not!" (Ahh . . . lame response number two. I'd almost forgotten about that one.)

"What about the guys?"

"They have no problem with it."

"Are you kidding?"

"They didn't say anything."

"Did you ask them?"

"No."

"Is Nili coming?"

"No, she's going back to Israel in a few days, her boyfriend is getting antsy."

"Nili has a boyfriend?!"

"Oh yes, he's gorgeous, I've seen pictures. He's a pilot."

"Of course he is."

"So she's just going to stay in Pokhara?"

"Yes, she doesn't know when she'll be able to get a flight back to Israel. Could be tomorrow, could be at the end of the week."

"But she's not coming to the safari for sure."

"Yes, she's not coming."

"You sure?"

"*Yes*!!"

"I see."

"Well, anyway, we're leaving tomorrow morning, so it's up to you."

"Do you really want me to come?" I ask in a final attempt to get some desire and positivity out of her.

"It's up to you, Iris. What do you want?"

Well I guess the first step to my de-freakage is accepting the fact that I'll rarely get the answer that I want. But at least I got the question. And if Iris won't provide me with adequate decision-making information, I will just have to find it for myself. *Victim no more!* I declare.

I breathe in some Nili-hating confidence and march up to the third row, where Yotam and the tart are playing rock paper scissors. I push her leg, which is inconsiderately leaking out into the aisle and shove up against her, making sure my fanny pack grinds her soft creamy shoulder.

"Yotam!" I bark.

He looks up distractedly.

"What?" he replies, inappropriately cupping Nili's rock hand with his scissor palm.

"You want me to come to the safari with you or not?"

Nili nudges him surreptitiously, but my gaze is so intense he is unable to look to her for advice. I continue.

"Because if you don't want me to come, that's fine. I just need to make my plans."

"No, I do, I do want you to come."

Nili is taken aback by his sudden sheepishness. At this point I couldn't care less if he means it, I'm just happy I'm winning this round.

"Are you not going to hang out with me in Pokhara?" Nili asks, a pout creasing her face for the first time in the history of perfection.

"I will, Nili, it's only for three days. I've just been planning this safari for a long time. You can come if you want."

Shit. This round is taking a downward turn. I nudge the fanny pack deeper into her shoulder, the zipper making an indentation in her arm. Feel the pain, Nili. Feel it.

"Iris, your pouch is hurting me."

"Oh, I'm sorry," I smile, Cheshire-like. "You're more than welcome to join us, Nili."

"*I know* I'm welcome. The safari was my idea."

Zipper punctures flesh. Nili winces. This could get ugly. I release before drawing blood.

"But I can't go. I'm on standby for a flight and—"

"Oh, that's too bad. Oh well," I say, chopping her sob story short. Yotam finally manages to unlock his gaze. He takes Nili's hand and squeezes it.

"Well, I'll be back before you leave, I promise. We'll have a going-away party and everything."

I give Nili a final zipper gash and stroll back to my seat, extremely satisfied with the outcome of the match.

Chapter Twenty-Six

Our safari huts are situated in the middle of a vast savannah, just like the brochure promised. If I didn't know we were in Asia, I would've sworn we were in Africa. We are the only ones present on the nature reserve, it being safari low season and all. Hey, more animals for us. Roaring lions. Mating giraffes. Hut-storming bison. All this and more would be happening very soon. (Jip, our safari master, said so.)

Jip is a somewhat manic fellow, a jiffy-pop of excitement, who could not be more thrilled to be our expedition leader. Poor Jip has no neck to speak of, while the rest of his body is of uniform width, shoulders to ankles. He is, in essence, a fleshy rectangle. His smushed face makes me think he was a boxer in his early years, perhaps famed across the Southeast Asian circuit. His eyes are wild, like someone who spends his days scouting dangerous animals. His enthusiasm is contagious and he speaks solely in urgent, hushed tones, as if the wildebeest were listening at all times. He brings us into an intense huddle for a pep talk.

"You go into wild today, you speak in whisper sound, never loud. We see many wild animal today, it very exciting for you. You like you see all day until sun is out. You bring water and speak in whisper never loud if not animal attack, very dangerous bad, bad, loud bad."

And with that, Jip leaps into the forest with us scuttling quietly behind him. It's dense and astoundingly quiet. The tension mounts as we probe deeper and deeper into the woods.

Every few seconds Jip intercedes with a very loud "SHHHHHHHH!!!!!!!" that would scare any animal in a ten-mile radius much more than our panicked whispering. I look around at everyone's faces: Iris is terrified, Yotam is looking at me with lust, and Udi is an Israeli version of Crocodile Dundee, pocketknife in hand, ready to strike.

Jip turns a corner.

"KARNAF! KARNAF! KARNAF!" he shouts, leaping four feet into the air. We all look at each other, not knowing what the hell he is talking about, when it dawns on us that he is speaking Hebrew. *Karnaf* is Hebrew for rhino, and once we realize Jip is a polyglot, our hearts stop. I look around in dread but see nothing. All at once we're a bunch of morons turning in circles, whispering *Where? Where? Where?*

Jip keeps shouting, "KARNAF! KARNAF! SHHHHH-HHHHHHHHHHHH!!"

I'm getting dizzy from all the spinning, but still see nothing.

"NO MOVE!" he yells hysterically.

We all freeze. Still nothing. I would think in this silence we could hear a rhino scamper away, but all we hear is one another's panted breath. I'm the first to break.

"Where the fuck is the rhino, Jip?"

"You scare it away, you scare it away!" he says with accusatory sadness.

"What are you talking about?" I ask, genuinely shocked at the accusation.

"You did, you scared it away, Iris!" Udi seconds.

"What? What are you talking about? There was nothing here!"

Iris and Yotam opt not to come to my defense. I can see where this is going.

"I guess I did, didn't I, when I yelled KARNAF at the top of my lungs!"

They all nod in agreement. Jip spits a fat lugey onto the ground.

"Back to camp," he declares in defeat.

"What?" Yotam says, finally opening his mouth.

"No more karnaf," Jip states with finality.

"But you said safari, not fucking rhino farm!" I retort, getting feistier by the minute. "Where are the other animals?"

"Tuesday, just karnaf. Tomorrow more animals. They all scare now."

I've never heard such rhinoshit in my life, but I'm in no position to argue. After all, I just ruined the whole day by my very presence. The group trudges ahead, leaving me to stare at their bobbing butts from behind.

Ass
By Iris Bahr

First recited at Abu Ghosh botanical gardens, accompanied by the Dimona String Quartet, Spring 1990

O glorious Ass!
How you appear before me
in your various forms

buxom butt turtlepant
heaving to and fro
east west north south
swimming reptiles on the
body titanic
chubby shoulders pumping
under massive red helmet head
Udi
rear-end non-existum
movements indiscernible
under spacious Thai fisherman's pants
chopstick legs
jut out
out
shuffling leaves on ground
while head stationary
atop bony shoulders
arms crackling swaying
disconnected from one another
acting independently.
Yotam
O! Yotam
O! Yotam
O!
Levi's exemplar
score score
ass grabiture galore
gayfully it sings
muscular and swift
The urge to run up and bite it
arises in the deepest recesses of my soul
but I contain myself.

Chapter Twenty-Seven

A hot shower in Nepal is known as a "bucket." One orders a bucket about two hours before one wants to bathe, whereupon one waits patiently in one's room until a small woman arrives with a large metal bucket full of scalding water. One then takes the boiling hot bucket into one's bathroom, where a small bucket of freezing water awaits.

After placing both buckets next to each other, one crouches and stretches both legs comfortably over them, swiftly dipping each limb first into the cold water, to numb the nerve endings, and then immediately into the hot, to soothe the areas damaged by the frozen water seconds before.

Supposedly, if one alternates quickly enough, the illusion of warm running water upon your body is created, but I haven't had that experience as of yet. It seems I'm stuck in the painful *you're fucking kidding me* stage of the learning curve.

I always seem to break down just when my vagina is chock full of blistering soap suds. Unable to tolerate the water any longer, I wipe the soap off with a towel, leaving a stinging yet fresh and springy smell wafting from my cooch.

Sensing that tonight Yotam is about to delve into my

magic kingdom, I make an extra effort to fully rinse my golden triangle, hoping to prevent any possible claims of lye poisoning against me later.

Success. I exit the bathroom and, as expected, find Yotam on the bed naked, bathed in candlelight. He's got Ravi Shankaresque music playing through some crappy speakers hooked up to his Walkman.

I'm nervous for the usual plethora of reasons, not to mention the fact that like Johnny, Yotam has fucked his share of Asian prostitutes. But he's Israeli, so it's okay. (Under equivalent sexcapades, Jews are safer, you see.)

Yotam descends masterfully. I come. Several times. He makes his way back uphill. I wipe his mouth nonchalantly with my hand, trying to sensually hide the fact that I have no desire to taste myself. We kiss some more. With great strength and agility he places me on top of him. The man is as hard as a rhino. How appropriate. And I'm relaxed. I'm actually relaxed. I'm ready. It's gonna happen.

"Where are the condoms?" I whisper, delivering the line as sexily as possible, which isn't very sexily.

He doesn't respond.

I try again, in a more playful fashion.

"Yotamush."

"What?" he groans, his mouth aggressively pursuing my left nipple.

"Put a condom on . . . I'm ready for you."

His rhino is now slowly creeping into my forest. I speak up, just in case his hard-on has somehow damaged his hearing. I've been through this sensory impediment act before.

"Yotam, put a condom on. Please."

"Just relax, Iris, I'm only gonna go a little bit inside, just a little bit, don't worry."

I may be a virgin, but I'm no dummy. "Just a little bit" means halfway up my pancreas.

"No, Yotam, I can't."

And BOOM. He's in. About three inches. Ouch. Pain. Joy. Pain. Panic. I leap off of him, and run to the bathroom in a fluster. If I get back soon, maybe he won't notice I've gone.

No such luck. By the time I come out, his boner is gone and he's lying there sullen. I try to snuggle in his armpit. He pushes me away angrily.

"I can't believe you fucking did that!" he says with a fierceness I have never seen in him before.

"Yotam, I'm sorry."

"You're so selfish! You come three times and you don't give a shit about my pleasure!"

"No, no, that's not it, I just wanted you to put on a condom."

"Whatever, my hard-on is gone, it doesn't matter anymore."

Yotam turns away from me. I can hear the disgust in his breathing. I stare at his fuming neck for a few minutes, then caress his shoulder gently but stop when I witness the hairs literally rise on his back at my touch. I get it. The man doesn't want me right now. I turn the other way, trying desperately to fall asleep, but his angry oxygen contaminates the room, and I hold back the urge to cry, puke, and slit my wrists.

Chapter Twenty-Eight

It's just been decided by everyone but me to head back to Pokhara early, due to lack of animals, and the fact that Yotam suddenly wants to see Nili before she leaves. That's my theory at least. I do not protest, still feeling like shit about last night. And Yotam knows it. He's had his Walkman on full blast since the moment we boarded the bus. I'm aching inside. The Beatles belt out of his headphones. I begin to sing along quietly.

"Love, love, me do! You know I love you."

"Shut up," he suddenly barks.

I am taken aback by his nastiness, but my reaction is, of course, to shut up. Nevertheless he snarls on, obviously not satisfied by my silence.

"How am I supposed to sing if you won't fucking shut up?"

"Yotam, enough. If you're mad at me because of last night, then—"

"Last night? I don't give a shit about last night! I'm talking about you almost destroying my friendship with my best friend. Going from one to the other. It's disgusting. Luckily, Udi and I worked it out."

Okay. Now I'm pissed. His audacity is so offensive, I don't even know how to retort. By the time we arrive at the hotel, my anger has completely replaced any feelings of vulnerability. I feel empowered. Fucker. I storm off the bus to my room and begin to pack with vigor and purpose, throwing my clothes into my rucksack with a velocity they've never experienced before. Fuck Yotam. Fuck Nili. And Fuck Iris for making a concerted effort to befriend the very people who alienated me from the start. That's not a friend. I'm over it. I'm really over it. Fuck all of them.

I can hear them all gleefully reuniting in Nili's room down the hall, their laughter bubbling amidst the sounds of hugging and kissing. And yet, I no longer hanker for their approval and their love and their fun group dynamic.

Iris just entered the room. Not that I care.

"Are you coming down for the going-away party?" she asks.

"No," I answer curtly.

"Okay."

She exits. For some ridiculous reason I thought my rage would have affected her incessant nonchalance, but I remind myself that my emotions do not wreak change on anyone, and therein lies the problem.

The drippy cry arrives finally, the unproductive tears just dampening my pain, like a rained-on Armenian newspaper that's now soggy and stuck to the sidewalk, impossible to peel off.

Heavy footsteps in the hallway. Must be Iris again, back to take her poetry book and recite farewell stanzas to Nili. Lo and behold, it's Yotam.

"Hey," he says, as if nothing were wrong.

"Hey," I reply, as if nothing were wrong.

"You coming down?" he asks, walking toward me.

"No" I reply, as if responding to a different conversation.

He leans in for a kiss. My lips are a rock. He retracts.

"Your lips are always so soft, Iris. Don't make them hard."

I say nothing, my lips still pursed in lockdown.

"Come on, let's go back to my room," he velvets. "It's our last night . . . I'll use a condom."

Of course. He just wants to fuck me. Unbelievable.

"You should go . . . Nili is waiting for you. It's *her* last night."

I stare at him with cold eyes. He gets it. He gets that I get it. I get that he gets that I get—

"Okay," he says and leaves, his tone devoid of any anger, disappointment, or apology.

I guess that was our good-bye.

I'm proud of me. For having enough self-respect and dignity to not utilize the long-awaited coveted opportunity to have sex with a man who doesn't respect me.

I feel in control.

I'm angry.

I feel in control because I'm angry. That's the only combination that works for me, it seems. When I'm not angry, when I allow myself to care and to love, I get clingy, freak out, and *then* get angry.

A festive cycle.

Can I only feel in control when I've distanced myself from everyone and everything to the point that I'm untouchable? That seems to be a crappy deal, too. That kind of control leaves me feeling just as empty, because when nobody's close enough to me to really care that I'm in control, the control itself loses any satisfying meaning or control-like qualities.

Maybe there's nothing wrong with me and these people are just all assholes. I like that option. All I need to do now is just surround myself with nice people who don't bring out my issues. Only one problem. Every person on the planet seems to bring out my issues. And they can't *all* be assholes, can they? As much as I'd like to think so.

One thing is for certain: I need a break from my own insanity, and since that involves less interaction with humans, it's time for a major change. A new destination. A place so overwrought with suffering, there's no way I'll be able to focus on my own. A place so repulsive to the senses, any horny impulse will be squashed before it has a chance to arise. A place so chaotic, it will allow me to find my inner peace, because I'll be too overwhelmed to do anything else.

India.

I adjust my nonexistent bra and head downstairs to Nili's going-away shindig. Besides the initial core trekking unit, there are about thirty other people I'd never seen before also at the table. Slut's got friends.

The clan looks over as I approach, stealing cryptic glances at one another that I'm too pumped up to decipher. I walk up to the table, plant my feet, and deliver the blow to Iris with zeal.

"I'm going to India!"

Silence. Someone drops a fork.

"You're going to India?" Iris asks, dumbfounded. "I

thought you said you wouldn't go to India if somebody paid you?"

"Well, I was being dramatic. I fly to Delhi tomorrow."

God, I hope I can get a flight. I'd hate to look like a liar.

Nili lets out a snigger, which to my delight, is received with perplexed silence by the group. Iris does not move, an odd grimace on her face. Is she pissed? Terrified? Indifferent?

"Can I come?" she asks in a sweet, high-pitched tone.

I can't believe my ears. Someone is actually asking for *permission* to join me! I never dreamed this would happen. Iris is pining after my company. Either that or she's afraid to go to India alone, what with the three Israelis kidnapped in Kashmir last week and that Dutch girl raped in Delhi in March. Which reminds me—I'm not against the idea of a bodyguard myself. And to be perfectly honest, I've grown quite attached to this lump of elevated language and asexuality, poetic traitor that she is.

I pause before delivering my affirmative response, relishing the tension, the stares, the further potential utensil-dropping.

When I do finally deliver it, I employ the very line that has haunted me since the day I left the little Akha village on the back of a moped.

"Come if you want, Iris . . . you're a free woman."

An old woman gasps in the corner.

Everyone looks to Iris for her response.

"Well . . . I'm coming then."

We both let out a sigh of relief, mine surpassing simple companion maintenance. You see, the power dynamic just shifted. From here on in, Iris is on *my* boat. *My* ship. *My* train. *My* tuk-tuk. From here on in, *I* run the show. *I* call the shots. *I* overindulge in redundant phrasing if I want to.

I turn back around dramatically, wait for a final spoon drop, then swing my sweet ass back up the stairs. Wish I could hang, gang, but I must prepare for my departure to the dirtiest, most poverty-stricken hell imaginable. Whoo hoo!

India

Chapter Twenty-Nine

Exiting the Delhi airport, Iris and I find ourselves without even a millisecond to acclimatize, jumping into a parked tuk-tuk so as to not be run over by the millions of Indians who seem to have "stampede" on their daily task list.

"Main Bazaar," I tell the driver. "Hare Rama Guesthouse." He commences a very cryptic horizontal-yet-vertical nod of his head, as if trying to cover all options—

Yes!

No.

Right.

Left.

Maybe...

I have no idea!

Are you kidding?

Of course.

Leave me alone!

Touch me here.

I'm hungry.

Good night.

He's wearing a traditional Indian sheet of some sort and his hair is dyed a striking cognac chestnut color (I'm thinking L'Oreal, but it could be some higher-end German line that comes in that tubey unattractive packaging). A large statue of an elephant dangles from his rearview mirror. "This is Ganesh," he explains proudly. The Indian answer to fuzzy dice.

The stew of humans, animals, destitution, and limbless children that engulfs us is all at once astounding, depressing, and fascinating. Any mental preparation I'd made for such visions of misery have quickly proven futile.

Our driver maneuvers us through the chaos with great skill and recklessness. As he expounds on the many incarnations of Shiva, he quite unexpectedly lets out a really loud fart that manages to exceed the mighty roar of the tuk-tuk engine. Iris looks at me and giggles. Lucky for us, the fart smell can't compete with the odors we're already dealing with. The driver continues to speak, soon after releasing yet another fart, only this time lifting his leg off the ground to ensure its proper dispersion. I'm beginning to get concerned. And with good reason. The second fart is quickly followed by an earth-shattering phlegmy cough that culminates in a massive lugey launch that misses my foot by less than two inches. The man is out of control. He farts yet again, lifting his leg even higher, then spits out another lugey. Another fart. Two more lugeys. "He's going to explode!" Iris yells. Faster and faster he goes, his movements getting jerkier and more intense: lift leg, fart, cough, spit, smile, speak, lift leg, fart, spit, smile. By this point Iris is on the verge of tears and I've buried my face in her armpit. When will it cease?!

"This is it," he announces, pulling up abruptly in front of a decrepit building marked HARE RAMA.

His legs come to rest on the ground, and with a deep breath, he shoots out a powerful line of snot that barely grazes his inner nostril on its g-force trajectory from sinus cavity to earth. This final display takes Iris over the edge, and she screams in dread, clutching my hand in terror. I squeeze back, opting not to point out the small chunk of Shiva shmutz that just landed on one of her tortoise heads.

One difference I've noticed between Kao San Road and the Main Bazaar, besides the anorexic cattle, tapestry vendors, and wall-to-wall hardship, is that nothing sensorial is left to mystery. No standing around going, "Hmm, I wonder what that smell is." Here, each odor has an actual physical manifestation to support it, usually located in one's immediate vicinity.

Iris and I are starving (relatively speaking, of course). The Aeroflot personnel on our flight into Delhi thought it adequate to provide us solely with an unpeeled mango, with no knife, fork, or even napkin with which to eat it. Go Aeroflot.

And so our first step after checking into the Hare Rama is the outdoor restaurant next door. Iris is very paranoid about the food here. Considering we can actually hear the *E. coli* dancing in the streets, I don't blame her. Nevertheless, I have no problem ordering a plate of fried liver and mashed potatoes.

"You're crazy!" Iris tells me.

"Don't worry. It's moomlatz," I reply, showing her the little MOOMLATZ! sticker on the menu. "You're not going to last very long if you don't stop being so picky."

Iris eyes my plate with dread.

"I'm not scared of this stuff. I grew up on brains," I say with pride, referring to the cow brains my mother used to soak in cold water in a Pyrex bowl in the fridge, much to the horror of my friends who'd go to grab a cold beverage and find a temporal lobe instead.

Iris orders a banana and a can of Coke, because apparently even the bottled water here can't be trusted, what with the locals filling up used bottles with contaminated tap and resealing them and all.

As I chew on my bison liver, I try very hard to not notice the cow that's taking a dump two feet away from me.

Out of the blue I hear the sound of a skateboard approaching. I turn around, see nothing, and return to my mashed potatoes. The sound gets closer. I turn back around. Still nothing. When I look down, however, I see a stump of a man—literally a stump—no arms, no legs, wheeling himself down the street on this board using his abnormally large head. Never could I have even imagined such a sorry creature. He stops in front of our table and asks me for money. I readily reach into my bag, when an Englishman sitting behind us leaps up and yells *"Cello Pakistan! Cello Pakistan!"*

Frightened, the midi man begins to wheel away. I follow him with rupees in hand. I place them on his board, choking up with revulsion and pity all at once.

The Englishman nods amusedly. I guess I have *Newbie India* written all over me.

"What does '*Cello Pakistan*' mean?" I ask.

" 'Go away to Pakistan.' It's a big insult to them."

"Oh."

"It drives them away."

"It seems a little harsh, don't you think?"

"Trust me, you'll be doing the same thing in no time. You start giving to one beggar, suddenly hundreds are upon you. There's no end to it. You're not going to fix India, you'll just end up getting all your money pickpocketed."

Well, easier said than done, I think to myself, as a young boy with no forearm heads my way. I expect him to ask me for money, but he just walks past.

I return to the table to find that Iris has ordered another banana. I plop down onto my seat, suddenly exhausted. I don't know how much of this tortured humanity and suffering I can take, let alone enjoy. The plan had been to reduce my state of hypervigilance, not increase it—to lose myself in an alternate universe and gain perspective from the less privileged world around me. But it is not perspective I'm gaining, it's a heavy pain in my chest from seeing all the debilitated, hungry, and handicapped beings around me.

It's the same feeling I get whenever I visit my brother's group home. Seeing the young boys in helmets, violently hitting their heads, as if angry at their deficient brains, yelling and screaming (in joy or agony, I can't tell)—the sadness is overwhelming, and I choke up before I even walk through the door. I tell myself, "They're not suffering, they're not even aware of their condition," but that never helps. Because *I* am aware. And as I sit there next to my brother, I fight back tears, embarrassed by my emotionality and weakness. I quietly watch the cheery counselors milling about, always in miraculously good spirits. My family calls them angels, and that they are. Unlike me, who wallows in tortured thoughts of these boys' fates, who manages to go beyond compassion, beyond empathy, and into full-on identification, these counselors don't have time for such self-indulgent bouts of despair—they have boys to take care of, to groom, to talk to, to laugh with. And they do so with pleasure; otherwise they wouldn't be able to do it at all, and ten boys would be wondering what the hell their caretakers were doing lying in sobbing lumps on the couch.

The point is, that same feeling is bubbling inside me here in Delhi. And I certainly can't spend the next month crying every time a young boy with no arms comes my way asking for money. But I can't leave India either. After all, I'm here to see this country in all of its emotional and spiritual entirety. I'll just have to deal with my inability to deal.

And have plenty of rupees on hand.

"Are you all right?" Iris asks, sensing my verge-of-tears state. "I know, it's not an easy place, is it?"

"No, it's not," I reply, and surprising myself, commence to tell her about my brother.

She takes my hand. "If it ever gets to be too much for you, I'm here. Know that."

A feeling of calm and safety instantly channels through me. This woman is destined for social work, no doubt. She's got the gift. And only twenty-six years old! I pray to attain even a bit of the peace of mind she possesses by the time I reach her age. Without turning into a geeky old maid, of course.

"Thank you," I say honestly, squeezing her hand. We must look like an informational video on lesbian communication techniques.

"How about we eat somewhere special tonight?" I say. "Somewhere new and not on the street!"

"Good idea!" she says, and we rush back to the hotel room before a group of local men reaches our table, their hands outstretched.

Chapter Thirty

We just found a new restaurant on the rooftop of the Shiva Hotel across the street. Apart from the bulimic rat that scurries past every three minutes, the vibe here is pretty fantastic. It seems that the backpackers who come to India are of a different caliber, and I'm happily encountering new members of the hierarchy. That being said, the impoverished surroundings give the Main Bazaar a hard-core summer-camp-in-war-torn-region feel, and I sense the hierarchy itself is not as stringent, the boundaries between the various classes dissolved to some extent.

Iris and I are at a table with a Dutch couple who just spent a few months at an ashram in Rishikesh.

Rishikesh. God, what a great word. What fun to say it.

One more time.

Rishikesh.

It's hard to hear what the Goudas are saying over the shouty laughter from a clan of super cool good-looking Israelis in the corner. They've come equipped with their own personal boom box that's currently spitting out speedy trance music. Jesus, they're having a lot of fun. Two really hot girls in sexy psychedelic outfits are dancing by the table, while the other hiptrippy members cheer on as the king of their clan, too perfect for the human eye, sucks on a large smoking device the Dutch tell me is called a *chillum*, specially designed for the potent Indian hash known as *charas*.*

My intimidated retinas watch from afar as the King sucks the chillum with passionate vigor, eventually exhaling a plump plume of smoke so extensive it manages to make its way across the entire rooftop patio all the way to our table. The crowd cheers at his accomplishment with ritual cries of *Boom Shiva!* and *Boom Bolonat!* all the while bouncing their heads to the trance beat with a festive intensity.

Iris waves the smoky air with her hands disapprovingly. I just sit there, enamored by this drug-embering phallus that spits out fiery sparks like magic. Kismet.

"The Goa clan," Gouda One tells me. "They go from one rave to the next, pumping their bodies with so much LSD their teeth rot and they can't see past the chillum stuck in their faces."

"They always seem so snobby to me," Gouda Two says.

The hot girls are dancing harder and faster now. The chillum is so fired up, I think it might launch into the cosmos.

"Let's get out of here," Iris says. "It's loud and I'm tired."

We walk past the clan on the way to the exit. I smile at the group approvingly.

"Boom!" I yelp with enthusiasm, promptly realizing nobody is holding up a chillum at this particular moment.

---

*The chillum is apparently also a favorite accessory among the indigenous Sadhu holy men who leave society to roam the Indian countryside in a meditative stupor. How convenient.

The clan looks at me with some confusion, offering me the chillum silently. It's still burning. My hand is about to reach out and embrace this happy group of exclusive souls who have obviously found a beautiful carefree joy and freedom, even if it is a mindless one. But Iris is already halfway down the stairs yelling my name. I give the clan an "I'm all set—I have my own chillum back at the room" slick nod of my head. They nod in semiconvincing understanding, and I leap down the stairs, praying I don't step on the rat on my way down.

Well, Paranoidpant was right. The liver I ate on day one has been rejected by my system, along with a lot else it seems, as I've somehow lost over fifteen pounds in under five days. I'm pretty sure I shat out my spleen last night. Which is fine by me. I've no room for any superfluous internal organs anyway.

"You need to see a doctor!" Iris tells me for the millionth time.

I don't really see the need. In fact, I've never felt better. I've finally attained the sexy backpacker gaunt I've yearned for ever since some English stick figures walked past me my first day on Kao San Road. Not to mention the fact that my skin has turned a deep brown, my eyes are a glowing charas hazel, and I feel generally sexy by international standards.

"I want to leave for Agra today," I state, already bored with the egg sandwiches and stuffiness of the Main Bazaar. Knowing how badly Iris wants to see the Taj Mahal, I don't expect any objections.

"How can you even get on a bus?" she asks maternally. "You haven't left the bathroom in four days!"

"Don't worry. I have nothing left in me to give."

As I say this, the digestive Cossacks ride in on horse-back, and I run to the bathroom yet again to evacuate the village.

"The East-West Clinic is the best in Delhi!" Iris yells through the bathroom door, holding up the Lonely Planet to page 47. Memories of green crumbled flip-flops come flooding back. And that was just Bangkok. Medical treatment in India probably involves leeches and celery root. But I know she won't stop bugging me until I go.

"Fine. Give me the address, I'll be back in a few hours."

I leave Iris to write her millionth contemplative poem about Indian suffering since we got here, and set off to find out what was left of me that's still functioning.

The East-West Clinic looks fairly twentieth-century, and I'm pleased to find the staff wearing fully formed footwear.

Before I even step through the door, I'm handed a plastic cup by a pearl-toothed nurse.

"Urine?" I ask.

"No, stool," she replies, pointing toward a bathroom door located about a mile down the corridor.

"No lid?" I wonder, concerned that we are located on some geological fault zone that will hinder my intact return with the poop sample.

"Just leave it on the bathroom floor," she tells me. Nice. I can't wait to see how many other people received those instructions. She disappears into the lab in the back with what looks like a pink timecard in her hand.

When she returns to me awhile later, the card is full of check marks.

"I don't know how you are even standing up," she says.

"What do you mean?" I ask, confused.

"Well," she says, showing me the time card, "You have: 1. amoebic dysentery, 2. bacterial dysentery, 3. two kinds of worms, and 4. giardia. That's why."

Wow. Who knew one body could support so many organisms?

"How do you feel?" she asks, still in disbelief that I haven't collapsed midconversation.

"I feel great!" I say, meaning it. "I've adjusted to the fluidity of my excretions and have embraced its perks!"

The humor is lost on my doomsayer. Her face goes sinister.

"You must check yourself into the clinic for a few days to hydrate and expunge the various toxins in your body."

Shit. Expunging was not part of this week's plan. We have to get to Agra soon before the weather becomes unbearably hot; we're crazy enough going to Rajasthan in mid-July as is. This is definitely a plan damperer.

"We will have a bed ready for you this evening."

"Okay," I reply, hauling my petri dish of a body back to the Hare Rama with the bad news.

I find Iris sitting on the bed, waiting for my return fretfully. I hadn't realized how much she really cares about me. And I don't think she realizes how much I appreciate it. So much for expressing our feelings to each other.

"What did they say?" she asks.

I smile at her nervous eyes and deliver the news.

"If we hurry, we can catch the seven o' clock bus to Agra!"

Chapter Thirty-One

The bus depot is a cesspool even by Main Bazaar standards. It's a miracle we even find our station. I must say the fact that over three hundred people are all waiting for our particular bus is causing me some concern. Iris, however, seems more focused on ensuring we have exact change. I love her for that. Always on top of it. Not once has she left me without toilet paper, or forced me to use napkins or other random paper products that happen to be lying within arms' reach of the toilet. Oh no, Iris always anticipates when we'll be needing something. And I can always rely on her to make our journey smoother. Reliability is a tremendous quality I never really appreciated until meeting her, but now that I've tasted it, I find it indispensable. Being with Iris has given me a certain peace of mind I've never experienced before, an ability to not worry about taking care of the world around me at all times, because I am being taken care of as well.

Many people are holding little handkerchiefs in their hand, no doubt to cover their mouths from the approaching exhaust pipe. As the bus finally pulls into the station, the waiting mass runs up to it, and to our surprise, shove either their kerchiefs or themselves through the windows.

By the time the doors open, the bus is already packed to

capacity, roof included. Nevertheless, Iris and I board and find an empty seat with a kerchief on it. I use it to wipe the seat and we sit down, already tired from the sweltering heat.

We are about to de-rucksack when a mustached Indian woman troddles onto the bus, her layers of fat oozing through the gaps in her sari.

"What are you doing?" she asks with a trusty horizo-verti-nod of her head.

Iris and I look at her, bewildered.

"That is my seat!" she barks angrily, slapping my arm.

At that moment the entire back of the bus leaps toward us. They proceed to jab our shoulders angrily.

"THE KERCHIEF! THESE GIRLS TOOK THE KER-CHIEF!"

"I'm sorry, we were not aware that the kerchief func-tioned as a seat claimer," I say with an apologetic crack in my voice. Iris, on the other hand, is getting annoyed.

"Cello Pakistan!" she yells maniacally. "CELLO PAK-ISTAN!!!"

Might be the wrong thing to say when angry Indians are poking you with their guitar-ready nails.

"GET UP!" they yell, louder now. "GET UP!!!"

I fear a mass beating is imminent. We begin to rise, hav-ing some difficulty with our twenty-kilo rucksacks still strapped to our backs.

"GET UP! GET UP!" they chant, nudging us more vio-lently now.

Suddenly Iris and I are shoved upright. Before we are able to gain our balance, the bus speeds off, thrusting us back-ward. We would have fallen over completely had there not been a mass of passengers crammed in behind us to pad our fall.

"HAHAHAHAHAH!" the crowd jeers, delighted by the idiocy of these two girls who can't even stand up when shoved to and fro by an angry mob aboard a moving bus.

We remain standing with our sacks on our backs for the entire journey, jammed into a windowless corner, engulfed by bidi smoke and hostile stares.

"Next time we take the roof," I whisper, preferring the danger of being tossed off a speeding vehicle than being accosted for disrespecting a hankie.

We've adjusted to the omnipresent abjectivity of existence here all too quickly, I'm afraid. As if the mind knows the soul can't handle absorbing the full extent of suffering, it makes it just another part of the landscape. That being said, Iris and I still nudge each other when a young boy with his arms chopped off (most likely to increase his begging ability) walks past, but we no longer go straight to our pockets to give him a rupee. Because whenever we do, we're suddenly accosted by a mass of men, most of whom just grope our breasts (well, Iris's breasts actually—they can't seem to find mine), sometimes even managing to access our crotches. Suffice it to say, it is an unfortunate acclimation, but one that is necessary if one wants to minimally enjoy this country, which is, after all, kind of the point. I think.

Upon arrival at the Taj Mahal, we quickly discover why tourists don't visit it in the summertime. Not only are the reflecting pools completely drained, but the whole place reeks of human foot, which makes it somewhat difficult to enjoy the architecture and mosaic wonderment. We cover the whole place in under twenty minutes, taking some feigning-awe photos before heading back to the hotel to determine our next stop.

I'm feeling odd as we return to our virtually deserted guesthouse. I'm getting a little lonely with Iris as my only source of company. It has been just the two of us since we arrived in India, and while I've enjoyed reading three Gabriel García Márquez books and half of *The Alchemist,* it'd be nice to have some other people to interact with, perhaps even a man to focus on. That was always so much fun. When there were men around, at least I felt like I was being productive. Like I had a goal I was working toward. But it's not even about goals anymore. I'll go so far as to say that I'm actually horny. And despite the fruitful nature of the last two culture-filled contemplative weeks, I'm ready to de-fruit.

Time is of the essence, as I must also factor in my weight loss, which has slowed to an alarmingly healthy rate. The brown pellets I got last night from the street pharmacist downstairs have worked wonders, and so I must take advantage of my skinny state before either parasites or full health return, the former resulting in my literal disappearance, the latter in a disproportionately healthy butt, which my friends used to assure me were just my "birthing hips." They could not explain, however, why I've had said "birthing hips" since I was four. Perhaps to ensure a painless birthing process, lest I got knocked up by a crayon during nursery school nap time.

"How about Pushkar?" I ask Iris, who's sweating and lying face down on the bed, hoping to somehow extract some cold air hiding in the sheets.

"Look at this photo of the Pelican Hotel!" I exclaim,

holding up the Lonely Planet to page 72. "It has a pool! And a cute blond guy next to it!"

Hope the photo's recent.

Iris lifts her head up with great difficulty, barely managing to give an acquiescent nod. But her willingness to depart is clear. The smell of curry masala chai oozing out of our sweaty pores has become unbearable.

We arrive at the desert oasis of Pushkar at midnight. The Pelican Hotel is silent except for an extremely rapid creaking sound from one of the rooms.

"Wow, someone must be having fun!" Iris says with a grin.

This being the first remotely sexual allusion Iris has uttered since the day we met, I'm understandably appalled. Sex and Iris just don't go together. Then again, neither do I.

The creaking sound is getting more violent. Suddenly, a tall, shirtless, broad-shouldered, cocoa-colored Israeli with a jet black fro runs out of the room.

"I need your help!" he says to us in a panic.

"What's wrong?" I ask, admiring his perfect torso.

"My friend David took some bhang lassi and he's never taken it before and he's freaking out."

"What's bhang lassi?" I ask innocently.

"Duh! It's lassi laced with charas!" Iris tells me, surprising me once again with her inappropriate knowledge. "I read about it last night. It can be very strong, and one should proceed with caution, preferably avoiding the beverage altogether . . ."

Before Iris recites the whole chapter verbatim, I follow big boy to his room to see the psycho in question. God, he's got a great back. And I mean *great* back. Wide but not mushy. Sometimes the wider backs can be mushy, but it's quite obvious that his is firm.

As if sensing my assessment, he turns around and gives me a shy smile.

"I'm Tomer," he says.

"I'm Iris. Nice to meet you."

"Enter quietly," he warns, opening the door with great care.

David is a pale, small-eyed fellow who looks a lot like Lenin. We find him jumping up and down on the bed, burbling, "WowWowWow," while licking his lips and snapping his fingers sporadically. He swivels his head sharply as we enter.

For a moment I lose myself in his enormous pupils. After briefly checking my teeth in their reflection, I proceed to attempt an intervention.

"Is everything okay, David?

"Wow. Wow. Wow."

His whole being seems to be emanating celestial joy.

"I'm going to die," he says.

"No, you're not!" Tomer counters.

"Wow. Wow. Wow."

Impending death is a glorious thing apparently.

"Why don't we go out for a breath of fresh air?" I suggest.

Just now, Iris decides to walk in. She sees David and widens her eyes in disdain.

"Stupid kids and drugs."

Mind you, though Iris is only twenty-six, she has the attitude of a crusty ninety-year-old. Needless to say, this conservatism is not what we need right now.

"I'm going to die," David says again, sounding a bit more concerned about the prospect.

"Yes, you are," Iris says flatly. "Why did you take the drugs, then?"

These two must be separated.

Tomer gives me a panicked "What is your friend doing?" look. I smile at him yet again, and then realize such a smile is not appropriate for all occasions. Turn off the flirt machine for just a wee bit, young lady, we have a crisis on our hands.

"David, you're not going to die," I assure him, with a surprisingly deep and soothing tone to my voice.

David's look says, "You must know what you're talking about, because your voice is deep and soothing." So I continue.

"Why don't you lie down for a moment?"

I ease his body down onto the bed, gently caressing his head, wishing someone had done this to me all the times I felt the world was going to end.

He finally comes to a full recline, squeezing my hand so hard I'm afraid it will break. But for his sake, I brave it with grace. I wonder if Mother Teresa is still accepting applications.

I stay by Lenin's side, softly stroking his cheeks until his eyes close and his breathing tempers. I can feel Tomer watching me in awe, Iris in surprise. I finalize my intervention with a papal forehead kiss, release my hand from his, and exit the room with quiet drama. Tomer rushes out after me.

"Thank you," he says in earnest.

"No problem," I throw back. "You'll get me later!"

Tomer smiles shyly. He has no idea what I'm talking about.

Thank God I do.

Chapter Thirty-Two

Pushkar is a shopper's dream. Rows and rows of seamstresses and tailors who can make you anything you want in less than an hour. I just bought three pairs of beautiful silk drawstring pants, all for less than fifty cents. I'm picking up another fourteen pairs tomorrow.

Iris has not fared so well, however, and is utterly devastated by the lack of zoologically themed fabrics available.

"Do you mind waiting a minute? There's just one more place I want to check," she says.

"No problem. I'll wait for you by the pond."

The pond is at the very edge of the village, surrounded by sandy desert and whitewashed buildings. Postcardy. The pond café is deserted, save for a naked Indian tot cradling a tabla twice his size. He's drumming with awesome skill for hands so tiny, his blackened nails occasionally scratching the surface of the drum during his more emphatic gestures.

The menu has two options: banana lassi or bhang lassi. Considering I'm not up for any Leninesque "Wow I'm going to die" revelations, I opt for the tamer beverage and lean back to watch the sun set behind the dunes.

* * *

The rhythmic drumming has put me in a trance of sorts. The magical lure of India is finally crystallizing before me. While it is not found in the deathstreets of the large cities, it is those very streets that prepare one to truly appreciate the country's essence. What else can come of poverty and suffering than the highest level of spirituality?

I contemplate this for a while and wonder if Iris is still searching for signs of biological life in the textile universe.

It is dark by the time she appears, with a disappointed look on her face and three bags of solid-color leisure suits in hand. Poor girl.

I beam at her serenely as she approaches.

"Are you okay?" she asks, somewhat distraught by my tranquil air.

I've not quite entered the realm of infinite patience, and am suddenly annoyed that my newfound state is once again coming across as an emotional mood swing.

"I'm great," I tell her. "Really, really, great. *Super* calm and great and peaceful and really great. Truly. Great."

She still seems unconvinced but doesn't argue, sensing that I might get violent if she questions my tranquility once more.

Back at the Pelican, Iris rushes to her room to vent her recent trauma in poetry form. I'm still in a happy daze of sorts and place myself by the pool, hoping Tomer will roam out shirtless again to ask for my assistance. What a joy to find a man in my midst once again—a challenge, a potential unhealthy obsession, an opportunity. It has been too long.

An hour later I begin to hear snoring from Tomer's room but can't gauge if it's two nostrils or four. My question is answered when Tomer exits the room in boxers and a crisp white T-shirt. Gotta love the newbies.

"David asleep?"

"Yes. Still tired from last night. How about Iris?"

"Writing."

"Gotcha."

Enough with the small talk.

"Wanna go back to your room, Tomer?"

"Uh . . . sure."

My days of beating around the literal/figurative bush are over. And so the minute we close the door I take off our shirts. We lie down and begin to make out. His kisses are extremely sweet and gentle.

The sound of David's snoring is not the most sexual of mood inducers, but I'm able to drown it out by focusing on Tomer's skin, which happens to be a lot softer than mine. So much so that I feel like a lizard.

"You have soft skin," he tells me, reading my neurotic mind.

"Not as soft as yours."

He laughs shyly before getting on top of me. He's huge. His body I mean. I'm unable to gauge his more pertinent size, as I'm too busy gasping for oxygen through my crushed lungs.

"Do you mind if I get on top?" I ask him.

"Oh, sorry, I didn't realize how small you are."

I'm sure he's hoping I don't say the same thing about him, but I'm too busy with my next move to bother with humor.

I jump on top of him and quickly pull his boxers down. Why not? I figure I have to see this puppy sooner or later. To my surprise, it is a nice puppy. Not scudlike, not peanuty or pencily. I may actually find it not ugly or intimidating. Wow. I'm so ready for this pseudo-virgin fiasco to be over with.

"Wait, Iris," he says, putting his hand on mine. No fear, my man. This time I've come prepared.

"Don't worry, I have a condom in my pocket."

"No, it's not the condoms," he says, pulling his boxers back up.

"What's wrong, then?" I ask, suddenly feeling like every horny skeezball I've ever dealt with.

"Let's take it slow."

Slow? I plan on leaving Pushkar in two days, there's no time for slow. What kind of time frame is this guy planning on?

"Slow?"

"Yes, I'm a bit shy. I'm sorry."

"What are you, a virgin?!" I jest, hoping I might disclose my demon under such favorable circumstances.

"Very funny," he replies. "I hope you don't mind, I'm sorry."

"No, no . . . it's fine. It's just that . . . well . . . I'm very attracted to you."

My God, I *am* every horny skeezball I've ever met. At least now I understand their frustration with this bullshit "slow" nonsense.

Sensing my dismay, Tomer begins to dry-hump me. The pants I'm wearing are of the thinnest grade Pushkar silk, and after forty-five minutes of said activity, not only is the silk damp, but it's also ripped in three places and a small bruise has formed on my inner thigh. There's just no way I can take this slow. We need to move to the next level, even half a level. I'm not leaving this room until we do.

I reach into Tomer's boxer flap, ready to venture toward

the unknown of all unknowns: the hand job. My first. What if I pull too hard and it comes off?

"Guide me," I whisper. The man owes me a bit of instruction.

He takes my hand and leads me up and down the ladder of love, mind you at a much slower pace than I anticipated. In fact, any slower than this and I'll fall asleep. Up. Pause. Down. Pause. Up. Pause. Down. Pause. This has to be the most nonsexual hand job ever.

The worst part is, he's staring at me the whole time, with such love in his eyes. Or maybe he's just relieved he doesn't have to gyrate up against a silken knee for another three hours.

Not only am I getting tired and bored, I'm starting to get repulsed. These sweet kisses. This tenderness. It's freaking me out. Too sweet. Too loving. Too much.

I close my eyes and begin to make orgasmy sounds, fake straining my forehead to perfection. I figure faster is smarter at this point and speed up my hand dance, going from a tango to a frantic polka. Please just come already so I can go to my room.

"Yes, Iris, yes. Yes. Faster. Faster."

Hey, it's your skin, my man. I'll go turbo if you let me.

Boom. He comes. All over me. Finally.

Artichoke!

I let go immediately and wipe my hand on the sheet.

Good Lord. It's still coming out. Was I supposed to keep climbing the ladder? I put my hand back on his penis. He spasms with a jolt.

Wrong move, I guess.

"Sorry."

"It's okay," he replies tenderly.

He smiles and kisses me. Now his breath smells weird. It didn't smell weird a minute ago. Odd.

I lie down for a moment, relieved that it's over. He lies down next to me, trying to take my hand, but it's stuck to the sheet with giz glue.

"That was amazing," he says to me.

There's no way in hell that could have been amazing. Somebody should ask his penis what *it* thinks.

I give him a tender kiss good night, one that I know will make up for my abrupt departure. I leave ambivalent, feeling like we both just experienced something productive but not quite satisfying.

Tomer has truly made me lose hope in my ability to ever be a functioning, loving being in the universe. I've never met someone as handsome, sweet, kind, and smart as him. And yet I am repulsed by his very presence. I think it's this whole being put on a pedestal thing. Maybe I hate it because I hate myself. Or maybe it's just creepy because it leaves me no room to fuck up or be flawed. Or maybe it's just lack of mojo and chemistry, although that would be the easy explanation, wouldn't it. Either way, I don't know.

What I do know is, I need to get away from Tomer before I start getting mean, because that's the only way I know how to push a man away. The route of mature disclosure of feelings is still beyond my reach. Yes, I know, it's just a matter of being more zennie about everything. And the good news is I was able to find that peaceful place—when I wasn't focused on getting penetrated. What a glorious five days those were. Especially the scruffy toddler playing tabla at sunset part. And let's not forget when I contemplated how extreme suffering catapults one into a loftier state of being. But now that there's a new man active in the mix, it's weirdness and panic all over again. Sadly, neither the man nor the scenario seem to matter, the anxiety will always rear its nasty head.

But I have not yet given up on men. Quite the contrary. There is one man who can help me. He is the one man who can truly save me, the one man who can teach me peace that isn't susceptible to others' negative or positive opinions of me. A peace that isn't dependent on whether I don't give a fuck, give too much of a fuck, or fuck at all for that matter. This man is clearly the subconscious reason I came to India. This man is the Dalai Lama.

Chapter Thirty-Three

Dharamsalah is a welcome respite from the sweaty hen-naed groping gumbo that is the rest of India. The Tibetans are a kind, soft people who walk the streets with a constant grin on their face. Just being around them has provided me with hope and inspiration. These people, in tragic exile, have created this haven where they can live in peace, true to their nature, with their spiritual leader just a couple of blocks away. I wish I had a spiritual leader who lived a couple of blocks away. I'd probably be at his house all the time, inviting myself over for coffee and biscuits.

Speaking of which, I haven't met the Dalai Lama yet, but I have seen his Mercedes drive by a few times. It tends to stand out. I've repeatedly walked past the several cafés, quaint temples, and the large building known as "the nice hotel where Richard Gere stays" in hope of running into Dalai by accident, but he's obviously more of a home-body. No matter, he'll be holding his weekly public session at his house tomorrow morning, and I'll be the first in line.

I have to admit, I'm a bit nervous about our encounter. I'm sure he'll discover what a disjointed mess I am the second I walk into the room. My wrist will be shaking so hard, he won't be able to tie one of those blessed red strings around it and will ask one of his assistants to do it instead.

Today is the day. Finally. I can't eat I'm so excited. Iris has decided to take some long, contemplative walk up a nearby mountain trail, and so with much eagerness I walk solo down the hill toward the Lama residence. The gate is guarded by one of the fatter locals I've seen, a Tibetan John Candy of sorts. He's sitting on a stool, smiling to himself. God, I love these people.

There is a discernible skip in my step as I approach. I try to contain my gush and adopt a more businesslike tone.

"Good morning. I'm here to see the Dalai Lama."

"Very good," he says, his warm eyes welcoming my desire for salvation.

"I'm very excited!" I blout, no longer able to contain my enthusiasm. I may have actually jumped up and down just now, I'm not sure.

"Where does the line start?" I ask, not seeing any other lost souls hanging around. "Am I too early? Am I too late? Was I supposed to buy a ticket or something?"

Okay, calm down. The man must think you're insane. I'm sure you're not late, it's seven in the morning.

"No, you are not late," he assures me.

Whew.

"He is not here right now."

Oh.

"What time will he be back? My schedule is wide open, I could come back in an hour—"

"He is abroad."

"Oh." I wasn't expecting that.

"Where exactly?"

"Tel-Aviv."

"Tel-Aviv?"

"It is a city in Israel."

"Yes, yes, I've heard of it. For how long?"

"We are not allowed to disclose his exact itinerary, I'm sorry."

"No kidding."

"Pardon?"

"Nothing."

"I can tell you he will be back in a week."

"Okay, great. Thank you, sir."

"*Namaste.*"

I can't believe it. Of all the bitter ironies, the mother-fucking Dalai Lama has to pull off the worst. He picks the one week I journey to the end of the world to meet him to go eat hummus in Jaffa. Classic.

What am I supposed to do now? I had planned my whole day around this man.

If I wait six hours I can catch the first showing at the movie theater on the corner. If one can call it that, really. It's more a small dark shack with five wooden benches and a small Soonyang TV set. I saw *Dune* there a few days ago.

Night has fallen. I hope I didn't miss the previews. I ended up falling asleep on a bench by the temple, only to be awakened by John Candy on his dinner break, apologizing once again for the scheduling mishap.

I slowly open the door to the movie shack. Smoke pours out in an aggressive plume. The house is packed. A chillum is being passed around. I can make out some mumbling in German.

I squeeze my way to the only empty seat in the middle row, trying to get a glimpse of the TV monitor. It's a black-and-white film, which I immediately identify as *Schindler's List*. As if the Dalai Lama's absence weren't enough, I was now in a Tibetan multiplex watching a Holocaust pic with a bunch of stoned Germans. Fantastic.

The girl in front of me is handed the chillum by her neighbor. The whole row commences a whispered conversation. I find it somewhat disconcerting but try to focus on the action on screen, which involves screaming women inside a gas chamber. The incessant mumbling is making me want to scream along with them. Of course, happyman Spielberg has decided to make this particular gas chamber the only one that actually did function as a shower, and once water comes out, the screaming women sigh in relief.

The mumbling has turned to giggling now, with the chillum being passed to the next row of Nazi offspring. My discomfort is getting unbearable, and I do everything in my power to hold back tears, even though I don't know why I need to hold them back. Oh, wait, yes I do. Even under these disturbing circumstances, I need to be liked by the very people I am now utterly repulsed by. God forbid they see me upset and think I'm judging them for their grotesque behavior. What I *should* be doing is standing up and yelling, "How can you behave with such utter disrespect!" like any other Israeli would. But I don't. I get up invisibly and skulk toward the door, wanting desperately to extricate myself from this alienating—yet somehow life-affirming—situation. While I could not feel more alone in the world right now, in that aloneness my identity is truly clear and distinct.

Well, at least the Jewish aspect of it is. Although, come to think of it, even that clarity is sketchy. I have, after all, never found cohesiveness within the Jewish identity either, having been a lone secular child among Orthodox, a Margaret among Deenies, a gypsy among her own people.

But the question is, am I really lost, or just flexible? The vast number of sociological groups in existence actually makes it physically and psychologically impossible to feel connected to all of them all of the time. One simply can't belong to all the groups, which is why most people just pick one and stick with it.

Lucky for me, however, my chameleon-like abilities have allowed me to experience all these different subgroups and semi-belong to them for impressive stints of time. Yes, indeed. My ability to adapt is a skill, not a flaw! A sign of strength, not of weakness and pathetic need. Well, maybe part of it is weakness and pathetic need, but there's still the strength part. The way I see it now, this floating may have its price, but the price is enrichment, fulfillment, confusion, at times misery and alienation, but overall a fuller life experience than those locked in their comfortable belonging levels in the hierarchy. And you know what? Fuck the Germans and their blond dreadlocks. Whoever heard of blond dreadlocks! They look stupid and ridiculous and Bob Marley would turn in his grave if he saw them. They need to show some respect for my people, my nation, my identity. Do it, woman.

"SSSHHHHHHHHHHH!"

The startled group goes quiet. They look back at their sudden schoolmaster. I glare at them with a force I didn't know I had in me. "SHHHHH!" I say again. They turn back around obediently.

I watch them for another few moments to ensure attention

is at a maximum, occasionally meeting a confused glance with a harsh stare. They probably think I own the place.

Once I've restored order and respect, I exit the shack with great pride. My people would be proud. All 245 subgroups of them.

I begin my walk back toward the guesthouse with an enjoyable newfound non–sense of being. As I turn the corner, the sound of faint trance music beats the air. Must be the Goa clan. Yep, I can hear their baked laughter interrupted only by strong intakes of the chillum, immediately followed by the celebratory cries of "Boom Shiva!"

Passing the café, I see them dancing and smoking, just as I anticipated.

"Hey, come join us!" they chime in sporadic mental unison, a dreamy invitation that no doubt stems from my being sans Iris at the moment.

"I can't, I have to get back to my friend. We need to pack."

"Where are you going to next?" someone asks.

"I have no idea," I reply, realizing I don't really feel like going anywhere anymore.

"We're going to Manali. Best full-moon party of the year next week, top of the Himalayas, DJ Tzuyoshi. It's going to be unreal."

I know Iris has been waiting in the room for hours, eager to hear how the Dalai Lama meeting went. She deserves my respect, if not my prompt return.

"Have fun!" I reply with a cool nod and saunter off. I can feel the men's eyes on my departing ass, which I know for a fact looks mighty fine in my purple silk pants. Take that, Goa Girls.

Chapter Thirty-Four

Iris is asleep in her clothes when I enter.

She awakens with a start.

"How'd it go?" she asks.

"Great. It went really great."

"I'm so happy to hear that!" she says.

We look at each other for a quiet moment. A strangely full feeling in the space between us, one of understanding, love, and acceptance.

She suddenly leaps off the bed and reaches for her bag, pulling out a pamphlet.

"Remember the Vipassana course we talked about doing up on the mountain?"

"Yes, of course." We had been planning to do this intensive silent meditation/self-exploration course at the Buddhist center for weeks.

"Well, they start one tomorrow. Isn't that exciting?"

It is exciting. The course is supposed to be incredible. Twenty-one days of silence and guidance and Buddhist chants and pure Dharamsalah mountain air.

"I'm going to have to pass, Iris," I say flatly, realizing what I'm saying only a beat later.

"You don't want to go?"

"Not really."

"Why not?"

"Because I'm tired," I reply, sitting on the warm spot Iris left on her bed. "Tired of exploring, tired of worrying about my fuckedupness. All this time I've assumed everyone was much more together than I was. But you know what? I'm pretty together. I may float in between groups, moods, and mind-sets, but I do so with skill. And to be honest, Iris, I'm actually beginning to *like* my pseudo-virgin status. It's unique. It's fun. It's fresh. My entire trip has been clouded by this search for some literal fulfillment by a man. But the void in my vulva has been penetrated so many times in my head that it's worn and weathered and needs a break. It's my brain that's become the whore, and it's looking to lead a cleaner life."

Iris stares at me, shocked and educated. I pretty much verbally summarized the entire personal journey I'd undergone in her traveling presence in less than a minute. It was the most I'd said to her since our fateful encounter at Thai World so many months ago.

I get up and start packing my things, neither sad nor nervous nor happy. Just packy. It takes about ten whole seconds to roll up my three pairs of underwear and sixteen silk pants, and when I'm done Iris is still standing in the same position.

She walks toward me, embracing me with tears in her eyes.

"I know I never really shared too much with you," she says. "But—"

"I shared enough for both of us," I say jokingly.

"I just want you to know that I've really enjoyed traveling with you, and I think you're an amazing person. You're smart, funny, brave, and mature beyond your years."

Why didn't she say this stuff when I was in a self-loathing lump on the floor, is my question.

"Thank you, Iris," I reply. Her eyes are a truly beautiful green in this light. "I learned a lot from you . . . and I enjoyed our time together."

"I better go to sleep," she says, reentering the bed. "I have to wake up at four A.M. to walk up the mountain."

I tuck her in, surprised at how instantaneously she resumes her slumber. I notice she's clutching her poetry notebook needily against her chest. I wonder if she's always done that.

I open the door quietly and step outside. The air is still and gentle. I stroll back toward the café, not quite in step with the trance music pounding in the distance.

Epilogue

My brief stint in Manali involved trekking up a mountain along with a hundred ravers, a Japanese DJ, two donkeys, and a generator. For four days straight, I danced nonstop on a Himalayan cliff, snowcapped mountains before me, trance bass pounding the ground beneath me.

It was in Manali that I officially met Yossi, the king of the trance clan, famous across the continent as the coolest man alive. Yossi transcended the hierarchy, in fact he was in a whole other category, reserved just for him and God. Never in a million years would I have dreamed of talking to a man of Yossi's stature. He was literally untouchable, always flanked by four Goa Girls who cleaned his chillum and provided other festive services.

But it was Yossi who approached *me* one day as I sat alone eating breakfast. He asked me to come to the full-moon party and told me I had a great ass. I didn't know what part of his comment thrilled me more, but of course I said yes.

It got to the point of obsession. Yossi and my ass, that is. At the full-moon party he'd dance up to me and say things like "You're not the prettiest girl here, but you do have the best ass here," before bouncing back to the clan to take another chillum hit and drop more acid. And by day three, he had struck my real name from his lexicon entirely, opting to just call me "Ass" instead. Every short while his husky voice would sound above the psychedelic din:

"Hey, Ass!"

or

"Ass, want some water?"

and my favorite,

"You have charas embers on your shirt, Ass."

Now as great as my ass is, and it is truly great, I couldn't get past having my entire being reduced to two bagel-like butt cheeks, and so after a few weeks of creative sexual exploration with Yossi that involved several failed attempts at intercourse, a lot of spanking, and a foot job (don't ask), the King and I parted ways, leaving me physically right back where I started.

But not for long. Thanks to a cucumber purchased at the local deli. It was such an obvious solution, I'm amazed it didn't dawn on me earlier. All those years of needless suffering. And I always did like cucumbers.

The specimen I chose was a risky one. Its size bordered watermelon-like proportions, but I figured that in the privacy of my own home, without the pressure of another human present, I could handle it. And anatomically speaking, if I could handle Big Green, I could handle anything.

I was right. Without the personal intimacy factor at play, cucumbering myself was cake. I was actually astounded by my ability to internally contain the entire vegetable, and scoffed at the banana skills I thought were so impressive only six months earlier.

Once I was confident that my vulva could comfortably contain large green vegetables, I was ready to proceed to the real hurdle: a human.

He happened to call me the next day. His name was Nir, and he was a pasty nebbish whom I hadn't seen since I was a teenager. I remember him being serviceably attractive and eagerly invited him to spend the weekend.

Nir showed up at my door with eight crisp T-shirts for his two-day visit and skin so white he deflected light. Not as attractive as I remembered, but I wasn't about to let that get to me. Not this time.

That night, I made sure to block every potential light opening in the room, citing privacy as the reason I was placing a shirt along the door crack. After a light snack, we started kissing languidly on my bed. After about fourteen seconds, I asked that he put on a condom and lead his way inside, making some joke about "self-service" so as to not reveal my inexperience in the matter.

Nir entered without a hitch and the act began. I let out an audible sigh of relief, which Nir interpreted as one of pleasure. He began to move and shake. My celebrated sigh of relief turned to alarm, however, when I realized I couldn't feel a thing. Literally. The man was pushing like his life depended on it, grinding, grunting, shoving, but nothing. I began to fear I had stretched myself too wide and was doomed to cavernous numbity for all eternity.

Turns out I panicked for naught. For since that night, I've reached new sexual heights, so excited by my very ability to have intercourse that it has become something of a hobby, encompassing a festive plethora of races, creeds, and sizes.

Sometimes, I actually cheer at the moment of penetration. This causes some awkward confusion on the part of the guy present, but his confusion quickly dissipates once he discovers there's a lot to cheer about. I've gotten good, you see.

And I'm proud of it. Because I've worked hard. I've worked long. And I've suffered a great deal to get to this point. The way I see it, sex with me is like being part of a miracle. And who doesn't want to be part of a miracle? I sure do!

Now if I could only find Johnny's number.

A Note on the Author

Iris Bahr was born and raised in the Bronx and relocated to Israel at the age of twelve, where she stayed until completing her military service. Upon her release, she embarked on a solo journey through Asia, then went on to study neuropsychology and religious studies at Brown University, graduating magna cum laude. She has since found success on stage and screen, starring in numerous TV shows and films, including a much lauded recurring role on *Curb Your Enthusiasm* (the highly memorable ski-lift episode), *The Drew Carey Show*, *The King of Queens*, *Commander in Chief*, *E-Ring*, *Strong Medicine*, *Star Trek Voyager*, and *Friends*, among others. She has performed at the world-renowned Montreal Just for Laughs Comedy Festival and costarred alongside Larry the Cable Guy in the nationwide release *Health Inspector*. Her first solo show *Planet America* received much critical acclaim and is currently being developed into a feature film, while her newest solo show, *DAI* ("Enough"), about the Israeli-Palestinian conflict, recently had its New York premiere at the Culture Project. *Dork Whore* is her first book.